WE
TEACH?

Martin Palmer

WHAT SHOULD WE TEACH?

**Christians and Education
in a Pluralist World**

BOOK SERIES

WCC Publications, Geneva

To my brother, Nigel,
who has taught me
more than I have ever been able to say.
Also to the two teachers who most moved me,
Mr Jenkins and Margaret Anderson.
Thank you.

Cover design: Rob Lucas

Front cover photo: ICOREC/Ged Murray
Back cover photo: Paul Herrmann

ISBN 2-8254-1040-3

Risk Book series No. 51

Printed in Switzerland

Contents

vii   PREFACE   *Clifford Payne*

viii   ACKNOWLEDGMENTS

1   1. WHY WORRY?

15   2. WHAT IS HAPPENING IN EDUCATION?

23   3. SO WHAT EXACTLY IS PLURALISM?

38   4. CAN WE HAVE DIVERSITY IN EDUCATION?

49   5. SO WHAT DO WE DO?

Preface

"Learning in a World of Many Faiths, Cultures and Ideologies: a Christian Response" — that was the title of a four-year project on intercultural education (1986-90) sponsored by the WCC Sub-unit on Education. It would be hard to find a concern of greater relevance and urgency for Christians today, especially for those involved in education, whether as professional teachers or as parents, pastors and other "non-formal" educators.

The project, directed by Martin Palmer of the International Consultancy on Religion, Education and Culture (ICOREC) based in Manchester, England, took up four major concerns, each focusing on a specific area:

— How do Christians teach about other faiths in religious education and what is the purpose of such activity? (Holland)
— To what extent is the Christian message as given in the churches a hindrance to Christians in understanding and contributing to a pluralist society? (Kenya)
— Is science and technology being taught in ways that are sensitive to intercultural values? (The Philippines)
— To what extent do secular religious philosophies of education challenge each other in intercultural curricula of education developed by the state? (European Community)

The findings of these research efforts were reported on in five issues of the project magazine, *Interlink*. But the need was foreseen from the very beginning for a more popular treatment, addressed to parents, teachers and pastors, in order to stimulate reflection and spur readers to action in their own churches and countries.

This book, written by the director of the Interlink project, attempts to meet that need. Its major thesis is that Christians must accept religious and cultural diversity as a gift from God, and must, therefore, take seriously its implications for education.

Clifford Payne
Director, WCC Sub-unit on Education

Acknowledgments

I owe a great deal to many people who have helped shape and create this book. First and foremost my colleagues for so many years in the World Council of Churches' project "Learning in a World of Many Faiths, Cultures and Ideologies: a Christian Response" — which for fairly obvious reasons was soon given the short title of "Interlink"! In particular I want to thank Désiré Brokerhof and Ari Zurmond of the Dutch project; Eugenio Gonzales and Nona Calo of the Philippines project; Obed Ochwanyi and Ng'ang'a Njiraini of the Kenya project; Pieter Batelaan of IAIE; Michael Shackleton and Jack Hogbin for their unstinting support to all the projects; my day-to-day colleagues in this project, Nicki van der Gaag and Palavi Mavani (now Patel); my "boss" at the WCC, Clifford Payne, whose comments on this text have made it so much more expressive of what we worked on for the four years of the project.

I also want to thank my colleagues in the International Consultancy on Religion, Education and Culture (ICOREC). To Joanne O'Brien, who gave me the confidence to write this book and helped me get excited about the ideas. To Liz Breuilly, who did her usual job of calming down that excitement and ensuring that what I wrote could stand up to some degree of critical examination! To Jo Edwards for her patience and interest. Finally, to my wife Sandra, a teacher whose patience, dedication and critical questioning never ceases to amaze and humble me, and to give me a sense of what it can mean to be a Christian in education. Thank you all.

1. Why Worry?

Seated at her imposing desk in her study, the headmistress spoke slowly and carefully about the delicate balance she has to maintain. The school is a Christian girl's school, but now part of the state system. "We have students from many different faiths here. The majority are Hindus, then come the Muslims; the Christians take a very small number of places and they are followed by smaller groups such as the Jains and Parsees. In our teaching during lessons, we stress the unity of all people. Then, during the lunchtime, we have Christian lessons which are voluntary — Bible study sessions and such like. These are for any who wish to attend — and quite a few do. But this is not part of the curriculum."

Thousands of miles away, the school hall empties of students after their assembly, and the headmaster walks back to his room. "It is very hard knowing what to do in a church school these days. What does it mean to be a church school, when over ninety percent of your pupils are Muslims? What do we teach, and why? It is very challenging."

These two schools, the first in New Delhi, India, and the second in Rochdale, Lancashire, in the UK, capture shared concerns. What on earth are we Christians doing in education these days, given the pupils we now have — given the sort of pluralist societies in which we now live.

These two stories could be repeated for many countries worldwide. In the wake of the vast missionary and revivalist energies of the last hundred years or so, the church has a major stake in education in many countries of the world. From primary schools through to universities, the church has frequently been the stimulant for formal education, providing both the physical buildings and the trained personnel. As national identities and national awareness of the need for education have grown, the church has become a partner and then, frequently, a donator to the state system. In many countries, the church still retains a powerful presence in education, while in others, it has been deposed from its power but still provides many of the actual teachers. The link between Christianity and education is a long, honourable and worthy one. Yet the goals seem to have shifted more in the last few decades than in all the preceding centuries of Christian history.

The origins of Christian involvement in education lie in Christian theology, language, metaphor and practice. Theologically, Christianity is at times an uncomfortable mixture of narrative and reason. Drawing upon the narrative models of the Jewish tradition, Christianity teaches through story. This is fused with the influence of the Greek rationalistic model where knowledge is to be gained, assessed and used. In its at times delicate balancing act between these two very different visions of teaching, the church nevertheless knew that education of one form or another was central to its purpose. Sadly, we have tended to veer more towards the rationalistic Greek model than towards the narrative, Hebraic one. The end result has been that Christianity has always been theologically and philosophically oriented by this Greek bias, towards formal, rigid structures of learning — that is to say, schools.

The theological influence has also been important in stressing two distinct aspects of education which to this day still dominate our normative concepts of education. The primacy of the first book of God — the written word of the Bible — has led to an emphasis on the arts/literature, and the exploration of the second book of God — nature — has led to an emphasis on science and investigation. Of these, it was always traditionally the sciences which were secondary and thus subservient to the word.

Christianity is often referred to as the religion of the word or the book. It is a very accurate description, for, being a revelatory faith, it is through the word of God that its authority as a faith comes. In faiths such as Hinduism or Taoism, the word is not the central source of authority. Its authoritative sources, writers and sages are much more personality-based. While Christianity has of course the personality of Jesus, it is his word which has been the primary source of authority. This is then mirrored in the scriptures, where the word of Paul becomes of greater importance than the actions of the disciples as recorded in Acts. The authority of the church fathers lies essentially in their words and only at a secondary level in their lives as exemplars. The Reformation shows that when the faith sought to return to what it saw as its authentic roots, it was to the word that it returned. The translation of the Bible is one signpost of this. The replacement of the altar by the pulpit is another.

By making the word central to faith, Christianity placed enormous importance on the ability to read and to understand. It also placed great stress on the ability to argue and debate, starting from certain given tenets and working out from these to solve current problems. Interestingly enough, Christianity's emphasis on the importance of the word has meant that from its earliest days it has been incorrigeably intercultural. First of all, the bulk of its holy scriptures are drawn from another faith — Judaism. Secondly, the New Testament was written in the language and thought pattern of the Greeks. And finally, it was quite capable of absorbing and using other, earlier, written texts in order to support or develop its own thinking, drawn from a variety of other belief systems, e.g. Aristotle, Plato and, in its apocalyptic materials, the mystery texts of the Middle East. This meant that the written word was given status and significance which freed the church from any fear that reading in itself was dangerous. An important first step in education.

The second aspect of theology which helped give Christianity a powerful impetus towards formal education was natural theology and its various offspring. Natural theology is the belief that through use of the rational powers of the human mind, through observation and study of nature, through use of the intellect, one can obtain knowledge of God and of the ways of God. This meant that the whole of the natural world, including human behaviour, history and thought, as well as the flora and fauna, were legitimate spheres for Christian exploration. While this attitude was for many years strongly infused with a basic sense of the integrity and inter-relatedness of all life under God, it nevertheless helped lay the foundations for the emergence of the scientific world-view. This is an issue to which we shall return in later chapters.

The idea that the natural world was a legitimate area for Christian exploration meant that the sciences could begin to emerge in Christian education, albeit that they were always to be understood as being subservient to the word. This is captured in the classic medieval statement that at the universities of Europe (all of which were Christian foundations), theology was the queen of the sciences.

To this day, languages and the concept-based subjects (often referred to as the arts or humanities) constitute one dimension of education, with the exploration of the natural world (the sciences) constituting the second part. The model derives strongly from Christian theological precepts and from the infusion of the revelatory influence of the Hebrew Bible with the rationalist vision of the Greeks.

Thus, at its very heart, Christianity is a multi-cultural phenomenon, committed, through its very beliefs, to the importance of education.

Christian language and metaphor is also strongly biased towards the teacher-pupil model. Many of the terms about Jesus stress his role as teacher; Jesus' use of the talk/story-telling style which the church, in a revealing phrase, often calls "sermons"; the whole relationship between Jesus and his disciples — all these further the model of education as being central to the Christian way. Looking inside the actual life of the churches, we know only too well how the teacher/preacher model is dominant, carrying with it the reaffirmation of the apparent God-given nature of education in the traditional mould.

From these powerful models, Christianity, from its earliest days, saw education as of vital importance in its vision of life, not just for the church, but for society as a whole. Thank God that it did, for without the church's interest, much of the wisdom and knowledge of the past which was common knowledge at the time of the fall of Rome, would have either been lost for ever, or retained only in the Arab world. As it was, Christianity's role as teacher of the West ensured not only the supremacy of the church in secular affairs as well as religious affairs, but also ensured the continuity of Greek and Roman culture through the so-called Dark Ages. A classic example of this at work is the story of King Alfred, called the Great, king of England in the ninth century. Born and raised a Christian in a very simple family, he became an ardent believer when a young man. He longed to study Latin in order to be able to read the Bible. But warfare and the affairs of state meant that he could only start when he was an older man. But start he did and he struggled to gain this vital knowledge. Once he had gained it, he then set about translating parts of the Bible into his people's native tongue — Anglo-Saxon — so that they might learn about God through the word. At the same time, Alfred founded schools, where the sciences were taught, and he translated or had translated classical philosophical and natural history books as well as books of history and poetry. For him, such educational activities were a natural consequence of both his faith, and his ability to put that faith into formal action.

As Christianity established itself in the countries of Europe and the Middle East, and particularly as it gained secular approval and status, it took the key role in educational provision. As Christianity became the official faith, so, given its all-inclusive vision of the word and nature as the two books of God, it took over all educational work. The spread of the monastic life-style aided this in providing both a place and community committed to education and to the production of books. In the monastic movement, one can see how the emphasis on the word (worship, Bible study, study of the classical texts of Christianity, production of actual books) existed alongside the scientific interests — for it was the monks who developed or extended the herbal books, the books of gardening skills and the rudiments of much medicinal work.

In the context of largely illiterate societies, where even the rulers could not read or write, the control exercised by the church through education was immense. Naturally the church could justify it as being for the good of the society. Thus, at the early formative stage of Christian thinking about education (the fourth to tenth centuries AD), the church saw education as one of the means towards the creation of the kingdom of God on earth. Educational control was an essential part of the vision of "Christendom" — a society or societies united in their loyalty and service to Christ, through his body on earth, the church. Education was thus a means to a great goal — as indeed it usually is. But it is important for us to recognize how the church saw the role of education in these earlier days, for later on it was to come up with a considerable shift in its understanding of the role of education.

The educational establishments of Western Christendom, in distinction to the Eastern Byzantine empire, were largely the result, not the cause, of the conversion of whole societies and areas to the faith. This remained the pattern in the Western church for many centuries. In the Eastern church, there was a different model. Perhaps a quick look at two different ways of converting peoples will help. In the West, after the eleventh century, the only lands within reach, which were not yet

Christian, were the areas around the Baltic Sea — areas which now form the Baltic states of Estonia, Lithuania and Latvia; Sweden and Norway and, finally, Finland. The biggest prize though, was Prussia. In order to conquer these areas for the faith, the neighbouring rulers established and used the Teutonic knights, founded at the end of the twelfth century. These knights were used as shock troopers who, by use of warfare, violence and military conquest, destroyed the old cultures and orders of society and implanted Christianity as a total social system. The barbarity of the Teutonic knights, indulged in the name of Christ, was long a scandal in the West.

In the East, the major areas needing conversion were always the lands to the north of Constantinople, the lands of the Slavs. The great pioneers in this area, during the ninth century, were the saints Cyril and Methodius. Their major work was to produce an alphabet, based upon Greek, for the Slavonic tongue. This then meant they could translate the Bible into this written form of Slavonic. Through the primacy of a non-military monastic order, the Orthodox church was able to establish centres of learning and of translation from which emanated the growing understanding of Christianity which enabled the countries and people to be converted.

In giving these two pictures, I am not claiming that the West used only conquest and the East used only education. We have already seen the example of King Alfred. The Celtic monks of the fifth to seventh centuries are shining examples of conversion through humility and preaching. Likewise, the Byzantine empire was not averse to using military means to ensure the conversion of a neighbouring group — but only under exceptional circumstances. What I am concerned to show is that whilst in the East it was normative for conversion to be at least partially accomplished by education, in the West, education was usually a by-product of conversion.

The slow but steady growth of education in the Christian world was of course mirrored by many other cultures. Islam is perhaps our best-known other example. The mosque as a place of learning has been crucial in the consolidation of Islam and in its spread. But other societies also had educational dimensions to their faiths, though not with the same missionary drive as Christianity and Islam.

While all faiths have been carriers of not just "religious" knowledge but also "secular" knowledge (one thinks of the great medical treatises of Hinduism, the alchemistic works of the Taoists and the astronomical studies of the Buddhists), Christianity and Islam were unique in being able to sanction not just the passing on of gathered information, but in instigating systematic developments of spheres of knowledge. Having said that, we have to note that both faiths have shown and still show moments of great concern about this process, especially when it looks as if a study is passing beyond their theological or moral control. Judaism is an interesting case in that, having been without a political base for nearly two thousand years, it never had to develop formal "state" education until the last hundred years or so. Instead it concentrated upon nurture, and Jewish learning has, of course, been known for its wide impact throughout the last two thousand years.

Under the aegis of the church, the sciences, law, philosophy and the arts were able to grow. At first, they were seen to be turning the pages of God's second book, the book of nature. But then they began to raise questions about the veracity of the first book, the revealed word of God — the Bible. It is this issue of the child outgrowing the nest that lies at the heart of the so-called battle between religion and science.

The gradual establishment of schools and education in Christian Europe and the Middle East took place over a long period of time. But that is not true for much of the rest of the world. At the start of the nineteenth century, there were Christian schools in Europe, parts of the Middle East and — as an extension of European society — in North and South America. By the end of the century, there were Christian schools the length and breadth of Africa, India, South East Asia, China, Japan, Polynesia, Micronesia, Australasia and Central Asia. In Europe and North and South America, what had become an education system for the elite and wealthy had broadened out to become an educational system for the poor as well. It has been estimated that between 1801 and 1900, Christian schools multiplied by over 10,000 percent!

Why did this happen? The answer is twofold. Firstly, the growth of evangelization. In the older Christian societies, this was evangelization of the working classes. Elsewhere, it was evangelization of countries either never before reached by the gospel, or "inadequately" reached. The second reason was the rise of Christian social action and concern — itself a part of the evangelical revival.

Let us look first at the old Christian societies. The discovery that large sections of their society were not Christianized, indeed, if the French Revolution was anything to go by, were actually anti-Christian, sent a shock through the churches and the ruling classes. It became imperative that these classes were reached with the gospel, partly to ensure their eternal salvation and partly to ensure that they did not rebel and overthrow the ruling structures. Thus education for the masses was begun out of genuine anxiety — anxiety for their souls and for the stability of the existing structures of society. It was believed that Christian education could bring the masses within the fold of the church and that they would then have a stake in continuing the structures of society. However, the social gospel dimension, whilst supporting the first of these aims, was in fact quite subversive to the second. It meant that as the church began to encounter the poor, oppressed and downtrodden in their own societies — especially the emerging industrial, urban classes — they began to see the consequences of the structures of existing society. To such reformers, Christian education was to become the means for liberating people from their ignorance so that they could begin to change society for the better. The tension between these different models often led social gospel educators to side with the rights of the secular state over those of the churches, in the struggles for control of the great church education empires, which marked so many European societies in the later part of the nineteenth century.

The second reason for the dramatic rise in church schools was the spread of Christianity through the missionary movements of the nineteenth century. This extraordinary explosion of religious activity transformed the religious face of the world in less than a century. Whole areas where Christianity either had never been seen before or had only existed in tiny communities, changed over the decades of the nineteenth century into Christian societies. The role of education in this movement was both crucial and controversial. It was controversial because many within the missionary movement, especially those from what we might now describe as the more fundamentalist churches, saw anything which was not direct evangelization as a watering down of the gospel. To preach Christ crucified was all that was necessary. To seek to pander to the material needs was to ignore the eternal soul. In places such as China, great debates raged within all the missionary societies about whether education and medicine were valid parts of the evangelical mission. For some, they were distractions from preaching the gospel. This led those who wanted education and health as part of mission to interpret the need for them in overtly evangelical terms. Both were depicted as being effective channels of evangelization and of sustaining and building up a thriving Christian community. It was not lost upon some that certain material benefits could be expected by those who were better educated than their peer group, and that this material incentive could be an opening for a willingness to listen to the gospel which brought such benefits in its wake.

By the 1860s and 1870s, education and medicine had been accepted by all but the most obtuse as being both good evangelical tools and as being essential for the sustaining and development of the emerging Christian society. Thus, tens of thousands of schools, hundreds of colleges and scores of universities were established in newly evangelized countries with overt Christian goals and the full curriculum as then being taught in the schools and colleges of Europe.

In its basic purpose and in its essential model of learning and values, the Christian school was truly an evangelical and Christian instrument. What was not appreciated was that the very forces which would wish to regulate and control such an overt instrument of value transference were being nurtured within the system itself. Just as the church found itself in Europe, struggling to keep control of its educational role in the face of nationalism (as in the newly created Germany of the 1880s) or secularism (as in the debates about the role of the church school in Great Britain after the first world war or in Eire after it achieved independence in 1921), so the church, often an arm of imperialism, found itself challenged by the very people it had educated.

The history of church schools in this century has been one of continued growth, but also of accommodation to the political, social and economic realities of the rise of the nation state and of independence movements. India is a good example of what has happened to these fine old evangelical bodies. Since independence, the church schools have joined the national education system, bringing in almost half of the schools which constituted the educational plant of the new state. In doing so, as a contribution to the new state, the churches saw themselves as real partners with the state. In the years since, much has changed. The churches' commitment to formal state education has not diminished, but their power has declined and the partnership role has rapidly changed. To begin with, most schools are now state foundations and the percentage of schools which are now Christian has thus dropped to only a small proportion of the total educational infrastructure. But more importantly, the curriculum is no longer within the control of the school authorities. As part of the secular state, they follow what is one of the world's most exam- and subject-oriented education systems. In order to cover the vast amount that they are supposed to teach, with the mind-bending numbers of students they have to deal with and with aging properties, the church schools are working flat out. The time for any specific evangelical or even religious work is very limited — and is now mostly in the form of keen teachers taking out-of-hours classes.

Nevertheless, the fact that the school has a Christian and thus wider-than-India focus means that many parents wish to send their children to such schools. This, combined with the tremendous devotion shown by many Christian teachers, has meant that these schools are not only popular and known for very high exam results, but they have also become, almost by accident, elitist. Move from India to Hong Kong or Singapore. Here, in the throbbing hearts of enterprise culture, it is the church schools which are the elite schools. It is from these establishments that the new leadership is emerging. At one level this is because the educational values and systems by which people measure success are, as we have seen, products of the specific thinking which emerges from a certain Christian world-view. At another level, there is no doubt that many such schools attract and keep devoted teachers who see their Christian ministry in terms of their pupils. But ultimately, one does have to wonder at the images of Christianity which are conveyed by such elitist, success-oriented schools.

Move from Hong Kong to Kenya, and the picture is somewhat different. Here, there are the elitist schools, but the bulk of Christian schools cater for the ordinary child of the towns and the countryside. Still very much a part of the state system, they nevertheless have considerable freedom and a role as partners with the state — especially when it comes to religious and moral education. While there have been times when the state wanted to control the church schools much more tightly, there have also been times when the state has looked to the churches to assist it in revitalizing the educational system and to provide moral leadership. The church schools of Kenya, as in many parts of Africa, have to tread a delicate but important line between these two poles.

Travelling to South America, one sees how the extraordinary transformation of the Roman Catholic Church in many parts of South America is reflected in the wide range of levels of involvement of the church in education. This varies from the elitist, to the development of alternative educational models, based on the base Christian community and fed by the work and ideas of great revolutionary Christian educators such as Paulo Freire and Ivan Illich. Returning to Europe, we see some parts of Eastern Europe where the church is being asked to play a key role in restructuring and rethinking education in the newly freed systems such as Poland and what was East Germany. In Western Europe, the old West Germany still maintains its Catholic schools and its Protestant schools, which have considerable control over their religious and moral curriculum, and we have the church schools of the UK where there is virtually no difference between the Church of England schools and the average state school, except for the odd religious service once a year, or an ethos which it is hard to pin down.

I could go on giving examples of the tremendous variety of situations under which the churches labour in education today. And this does not even begin to touch upon the very high number of Christians to be found in formal state education, outside church schools. The point I want to make from all this is that the churches' involvement with formal education is the area of its greatest impact on the secular structures of our world. Through the existence of church schools, the churches are in touch with more people outside the church community than through any other single activity. Tens of millions of children and, through them, hundreds of millions of parents, grand-parents and others, look to the church for education. Yet of these numbers, perhaps less than a quarter are practising Chris-tians, and in some schools, like the ones in New Delhi and Rochdale which were introduced at the beginning of this chap-ter, the number might be less than 2 percent.

So those who argued that the church in education was engaged in the most enormous evangelical field imaginable were right. Except that that function, save in a very limited sense of witness, is now dead or dying. The churches no longer look to their schools to be a field of evangelism. The state forbids it in many places; commonsense argues against it in others; in yet other places, those in charge see themselves as having a different witness to give these days — not at variance with much of the heart of Christianity, but not specifically Christian — the witness to equality, to justice, to peace, to anti-racism or to the values of mutual respect between peoples, creeds and races.

So what do we mean when we talk about Christian schools or Christians in education today?

Except in those quarters of the church where the painful lessons of the past have yet to be fully appreciated, the church in education is no longer the evangelist working for a personal faith in Christ. The nineteenth-century missionary model is either dead or moribund. Likewise, in many places around the world, the church school as a harbinger of the kingdom of God — a place of preparation for citizens of a new "Christendom" — is no longer a viable concept. To many looking in from the outside, most church schools and much of the involvement of the churches in education, are nothing more than a historical legacy. They are not seen as relevant for a modern, increasingly secular society. Within the churches, there are few who can articulate a clear and distinct role for the church in education. It seems as if, with the demise of the older raison d'etre — the building up of a Christian society or the actual job of evangelization — the church school and the church in education are now confused and unclear about their role, place or purpose. In many ways the situation reflects all the uncertainties of formal education — with the added com-plication introduced by a memory of its specific past.

It might seem also that the final *coup de grace* to the church in education has been the rise of multi-cultural societies or the recognition of the fact that many societies have always been multi-cultural. The argument usually runs thus: in a situation where a variety of cultures and faiths are to be found in our schools, it is no longer appropriate for the churches to have a key role in providing education. The corollary of this is that, therefore, the secular state needs to take over all education because it is "neutral", or that each faith or cultural community should be encouraged and aided to develop its own school system, adhering to certain basic educational norms laid down by the state.

The rise of the idea of multi-cultural education is probably the most serious threat to the churches' understanding of their role in education since the rise of nationalism in the 1870s. In terms of a challenge to the purpose rather than just the practice of Christianity in education, it is the most serious threat since the church won state approval under Constantine in the early fourth century. For what the issues of multi-cultural education raise is whether the vision and eschatalogical (final goal e.g. the kingdom of God) purpose of the church in education can still be deemed valid or not.

As we have seen, the church was always involved in education because it had a long-term vision of where it wanted humanity to go. It was involved in education as a means to the goal of a Christian society. When the church was either coterminous with the state or was converting areas and groups to the faith, then it could legitimately identify its vision of the future with that for the whole society. But now that there are a multitude of visions and of understandings, religious, ideological and economic, why should the church be allowed to use its historical presence in education to further one view, especially when it is a view which is often not shared by the majority of its own pupils in the schools?

Internally, Christianity has also been undergoing one of the most radical reassessments of its own beliefs. The recognition of the role of Christianity in imperialism and in the oppression of peoples; the emergence of women's rights; the awareness of racism; the quest for social and economic justice; the recognition of the faith's complicity in environmental destruction; the

14

indigenization and contextualization of the gospel — the list is long — have meant that Christianity is no longer as confident as it was about what it wants anyway! Perhaps the greatest challenge it faces is to find a meaning and purpose for itself within the context of pluralism — religious, cultural, economic, political and social.

However, it is not only the church which has had to undergo some painful reassessments and re-evaluations. Formal education has also been through a period of greater questioning than ever before — and in the process has had to shed a great many illusions about what it can, should or ought to do, not least, as with the church, in a situation of pluralism.

2. What Is Happening in Education?

In a book of this size, written for a worldwide readership, it is obviously impossible to do justice to the sheer range and diversity of educational situations and philosophies we have today. Therefore, in this chapter I shall be looking more at the overall assumptions of what one might call *formal*, state, secular education, within which so much of Christian involvement in education finds itself. The picture I am about to paint, as with the picture in the preceding chapter on the churches, will be broad and sweeping, but with, I hope, a few points of specific reference which will help ground it.

The greatest problem with writing about education is that everyone thinks they know about education because, after all, they spent nine, ten, twelve, fifteen — whatever the number may be — years in it themselves! I am reminded of the comment of Mrs Golda Meir, former prime minister of Israel. When asked if she ever received advice from the people of Israel, she said, yes, of course, because she had at least four million people who knew they should be prime minister, not her!

On the shoulders of education, great dreams are heaped. It is always education which is either to blame for the moral decline of a nation (usually as perceived by those in power) or it is education which is going to save us all from moral decline. In the UK, after the 1981 race riots in many cities, the then secretary for education in Mrs Thatcher's government went on TV to say that the reason for the riots was simple. It was the fault of education and, in particular, the failure of teachers of religious education. So that was why it happened!

In the countries newly emerging from the Soviet Union and the Eastern bloc, the hopes being pinned upon education are enormous and largely unrealistic. In the USA, the expectations of education to solve the country's drugs problem, drink problem, smoking problem — you-name-it problem — have meant vast sums being spent on utterly unobtainable goals.

What all this points to is that education is not about facts and knowledge, but about values. This is why states load the goals of education with all the value expectations which the society would like to have, but which it does not have. The question is, can education provide or raise up values which the actual society does not have, has abused too greatly, or actually cannot sustain?

Education is always about values and thus it is always about ideology and goals, about vision and about human nature. One great debate amongst educators is, can education actually change a society, or can it only reflect the sum-total of what the society is?

In the heyday of the late nineteenth century, it was genuinely believed that the world was getting better. Progress was obvious on all fronts. More and more useful things were being invented; more and more parts of the world were "opening up"; there were more schools, more education; more knowledge. The late nineteenth century could even see this progress as either being God-given or as a part of natural law. In many hymn books around the world you will still find that great hymn to progress "God is working his purpose out as year succeeds to year". In the secular and scientific world, Darwin's theories were used to support a progress model of evolution, which it has taken biology decades to discard as false. Within such an optimistic world-view, education found a very convenient niche. It was part of the process of progress and of enlightenment. Through education, the benefits of civilization and the benefits of knowledge would be spread worldwide. Once people were educated, they would know what was good and right for themselves. They would be able to play a useful role in society. Through education, the world could at last rise to the level of the intellectual and leave behind the mundane world of the material. With everyone becoming reasoning, reasonable people, progress and peaceful development were bound to come about. It was just a matter of time.

The shock of the barbarity, pointlessness and violence of the first world war shattered this image for many. Progress was not inevitable. Human nature was not improving. Education failed to prevent abuse. For example, the theologian Karl Barth wrote of his shock when he saw his great liberal teachers march happily off to war in 1914. The illusion of progress died on the battlefields of Flanders as surely as did the hundreds of thousands of men and women. Much of the consequent history of educational thinking has been an attempt to make sense of the death of that illusion or to find new ways to express the high hopes which once rode alongside the idea of progress.

The results are diverse and many, but perhaps can be put into a number of basic categories.

Firstly, there was the growth of concern for the child as the focus and purpose of education. Traditional models saw the child as a blank sheet or an empty vessel to be filled up with knowledge, facts and information. There was certain information which the child needed and a certain type of product was required by society from the schools. The child-centred model turned this on its head and stressed the child as a unique individual, with interests, a history, and a social context beyond the school, which all helped form the child. For educators looking for a new model of purpose, the individual development of the uniqueness of the child offered one very attractive way forward. However, two different interpretations of this child-centred model have emerged — what could be called the "for the child's sake" and "for the society's sake". "For the child's sake" sees the goal of education as being the fullest development of the child, almost regardless of what society needs. Many experimental schools, such as those of Rudolf Steiner, have developed this approach. The sole focus and purpose is to bring the child to her or his fullest level of potential growth.

The "for the society's sake" approach takes the need to start with the child and to move out from that, but assumes that the child is still being made fit for a functional place in society. Thus, the child-centred approach in this instance is simply finding the best way to engage the child and to draw the child into what are in effect traditional educational goals.

The second major category is the growth of meritocratic education. The massive increase in educational opportunities over the last hundred years has led to the production of many people who disdain manual work and see education as being a road to the comforts and income of the office job. Progress feeds this with ideas about the office world running the manual world — and of the manual world being phased out by the development of more and more wonderful machines. The results of this type of meritocracy are familiar to all from the majority world — the drift to the cities; the decline of traditional crafts and skills; the rise in unemployment and the increase of corruption in the white-collar world. The demands of many newly emerging societies for skilled workers fed the rise of meritocracy, and education was seen as the great leveller — the place where, if you had it in you, you could succeed and the world became your oyster. For many in education, not least for many Christians, this fitted well with older models of education as being the preserve of the elite. It also dealt with the question of progress because, following the dictum of "survival of the fittest", only those able to progress can make it.

Partially in response to this, and also because of the emerging actual needs of societies, vocational education arose as the third of these categories. That is based on the idea that education is not just about information, nor just about exams, but is necessary to prepare children and young people to play a meaningful role in their countries. Often this form of education is seen as being a less important form of education than that which is elitist, exam-oriented and meritocratic. Experiments such as the village poly-technics of Kenya or the practical and vocational dimensions of Chinese state education, were not really taken seriously by the other schools or by society at large. Vocational training also becomes a tool in societal control if sufficient care is not taken. The idea emerges that there are the "academic" children, and then the rest. The rest are thus given vocational training to make them useful "hands" for the factory or farms. The fact of the matter is that vocational training at its best is as essential for the "academic" child as it is for the less academically bright.

The fourth response is what might best be described as the overtly ideological response. This takes education to be the main tool of an ideology or world-view which it is seeking to impose on the people. Apartheid education in South Africa is one example. Through the very structures and values espoused by the education system, the ruling party seeks to impose its ideology on people and strengthen its political base. A similar phenomenon was to be observed in countries such as Romania or Czechoslovakia before the revolutions — and is still current in some sectors to this day. The total subjection of education to ideological goals is not just limited to secular ideologies. The rise of fundamentalism in Christianity, Islam and Judaism has meant that there are groups actively seeking to develop educational systems and curricula in which everything, from the size of classes to the choice of subjects and the way they are taught, is shaped quite deliberately by the belief system of the parents.

The fifth model is what one might describe as benign state education. This has long since given up trying to have an overall vision, and seeks to fuse the meritocratic with the vocational, in the service of vague goals such as personal happiness or prosperity. The United States of America is an interesting example of a society which, in part, has abandoned a straight ideological system — Americanization of all regardless of background — and where a benign model has now taken over. The original ideal which fuelled the US educational system was that of the melting pot. It was to be in the schools that the various cultures, peoples, tongues, races and creeds were to be levelled out and ultimately melted away. Through education, all people, no matter what their social, economic or cultural background, would find equal opportunities and openings. When this collapsed inwards under the pressure of the protests of the 1960s, the resurgence of cultural identities and the manifest failure of the system to deliver what it had promised to many within certain ethnic, cultural and economc sub-groups, the state was at a loss. What could take the place of the levelling, melting-pot ideology? The answer differs from place to place, but in many cases seems to consist of a variety of ideas fusing elements of the child-centred individualist approach and vague concepts of "happiness" and general wellbeing. But the model still finds it difficult to handle those who do not or cannot find a place easily within such a system.

Another example of a society moving from one ideological system to a more diffuse one is the Philippines. Originally, the Philippines education service was desperately trying to imitate American, Western values. Its implicit assumption was that the West had invented everything of use or significance and that the materialist, consumer world-view was normative. Since the overthrow of Marcos, major steps have been taken to break the monocultural model of education by, among other measures, the introduction of the wider use of Filipino. In 1985, the government formally announced the establishment of a new high-school curriculum where all subjects except maths and the sciences would be taught in Filipino. This clearly indicated the extent to which the government is still caught between two different ideological positions. On the one hand, it wants to provide education in the people's language, not in the language of the "oppressor". But on the other hand, it wants still to keep itself in what it sees as being the mainstream world, by teaching the "serious subjects" in English. The system thus being proposed and developed fails to address the deeper ideological issues left over from the past regime, while abandoning enough of the old structures to leave people unsure as to whether they are coming or going.

The sixth category is another variant on the society-child axis. This is the skills model. Put crudely, this approach says, you go to school to study in order to learn how to learn! The basic notion is that everyone needs certain key skills in order to be able to function in modern society. These skills are usually defined by governments as reading, writing and arithmatic — plus a few social skills, such as mixing and working well with people. Educators usually like to talk more about skills such as fluency in language and the ability to argue a case, creative skills such as art or drama, knowing how to work with basic maths rather than learning all the laws of geometry, and acquiring skills of living and working with people of different backgrounds. This is education for the future, but with a very undefined vision of the future.

Often, in reality, these six categories do not exist in isolation. In many countries of the world, a mixture of these categories is at work. One also has to distinguish between what is official policy, and what actually happens in schools. The key role of adequate funding, in-service training, initial training and support also profoundly affect the ability of any of these categories to function normally. It is probably true to say that there are very few countries where just one of these categories is even official policy. In most countries, a fusion between bits and pieces of these categories is the norm. This makes the task of those who wish to understand what education is about even more difficult. What exactly is one addressing as an educational model and thus as an educational method in any given country? The answer is not clear. It is assumed that somehow, out of this mixture, children will develop, society will continue and the right people will receive the appropriate training. In actual fact, most children are poorly served by their education and it is usually the case that it comes down to the personal skills and the personality of the teacher for a child to really benefit from education. In this mixed context, the vexed question of pluralism adds yet another disturbing factor, as we shall see later.

In theory, the church or the Christian in education can find a place within nearly all of these systems. It depends upon the kind of Christianity we are talking about. In practice, the bulk of Christian activity in education falls into the child-centred, the meritocratic and the benign state approach, with substantial interests in the vocational and occasional involvement in the ideological.

The difficulty for both the church and the state is, what vision of the future ought we to be working on?

The models described above are all currently at work in the world. But with the exception of the ideological model, the rest do not actually articulate a clear set of values, beliefs and norms upon which the future society is expected to be built. As we have seen earlier, this was one of the main motivations of the Christian to become involved in education, and of the state to establish universal education. Once this shared goal has disappeared, what exactly are we educating children for? In recent years, it has been assumed in the West that the benign, liberal tradition would effectively neutralize or resolve through patience the dilemmas of, say, a pluralist society. This has not happened and now the liberal educational world finds itself wondering what values it can appeal to which will be honoured by all. The result is that those groups who can offer a clear set of values are gaining in popularity and power.

One problem has been that many have tried to argue that education should exist for its own sake. It is a fine idea, but ultimately meaningless. Education is about values and skills. The kind of values and skills it espouses cannot be summed up as just being about education. They are about how to live in community; how to develop one's own talents; how to plan for the future; how to respond to crises, and so on. All these assume and need a wider framework of a society and its specific values. The question therefore should not be whether education can exist for its own sake, but under what terms and for what ends does education exist? In a pluralist society, this is a hard question to answer.

The reality of the situation is that even where intercultural education is now formally part of the curriculum, the actual practice favours, supports and encourages the majority culture at the expense of minority cultures. Take a very simple example. The term used in most European countries to describe pluralistic education is either multi-cultural education or inter-cultural education. But there is an immediate problem. Why use the word "culture"? For most of the minority groups in Europe today, it is faith, not culture, which is the major dividing block or potential dividing block between them and the majority population. It is being a Muslim or a Jew, a Hindu or a Sikh, which marks them off. In Islamic society, Hindu society and so forth, the centre of meaning is found in the faith, and this is often at variance with the Western idea of "culture". Thus in using the word "intercultural" the West is imposing a model of society and of values which it has arrived at in a post-Christian, supposedly secular society, upon people for whom such ideas are, if not unacceptable, at least somewhat meaningless. It is saying that culture is the key, not faith. This is already to erect a barrier of misunderstanding and to impose a model of reality upon people for whom such an idea is unthinkable or irrelevant.

The encounter with pluralism has raised many questions for both the state and the church and for education. They are not comfortable questions, nor are there easy answers to them. The promise and the threat inherent within pluralism, within acknowledged pluralism, are considerable. Yet pluralism is here to stay and is now more widespread and more widely acknowledged than at any time in history. The question is, what does it mean for us if we are Christians, if we care about or are involved in education, and if we sincerely hope to see our world become a more stable and bearable place for all to live in?

3. So What Exactly Is Pluralism?

It is doubtful if, in the last two thousand years, there has ever been a major country which was not intercultural. Take the imperial China of 2000 years ago. Whilst most of its population was Han Chinese, there were always the aboriginal peoples who had been absorbed into the growing empire; there were the traders from as far away as the Roman empire. There were the mercenary troops from the Mongol tribes to the north as well as visitors and traders from the peoples to the south.

The United Kingdom has a long history of intercultural life. Two thousand years ago there were many different tribal groupings; there were Phoenician traders living and trading in Cornwall. Roman traders and merchants were already established in certain areas of southern England. With the coming of the Roman empire, people from all corners of the Roman empire lived and died in Britain. Jews settled in the cities and practitioners of many different Middle Eastern religions, including Christianity, came and practised their beliefs.

Even where we can identify a culture which was isolated from other cultures and belief systems, we would still find different cultures. The difference in cultural patterns between the ruling elite and the poorest of the poor can only be adequately expressed in terms of two cultures. It is interesting that the term "two nations" used to describe the two cultures of the ruling and the ruled in Britain in the nineteenth century was coined by a converted Jew, the then prime minister Disraeli. He knew what a different culture looked and felt like.

So why is it that the phenomenon of pluralism, of interfaith and intercultural encounter, has only really emerged as an issue in the last few decades for so many societies in the world?

The first thing to realize is that while many of us are aware of pluralism now, there were other times in history when pluralism was not just a fact of life but also debated. Two examples will suffice to show that this is not new, just the scale of it is new.

In the China of Kubla Khan (thirteenth century AD), the intercultural mix was extraordinary. The ruling class was not Chinese but Mongolian. Many of these were Nestorian Christians, others were Shamanists, yet others Buddhists and an increasing number were converting to Islam. The Chinese population itself was composed of different ethnic groups who saw themselves as Chinese in opposition to the Mongolian rulers. In this Chinese population, many were Buddhists, others were Confucians while yet others espoused Taoism. A few were Muslim and a few were Christians or Manichees. To the court at Khan-baliq (now Beijing), came envoys from the Russian steppes, from Egypt, from India, from Japan and most other parts of Asia. Here religions and cultures rubbed against each other. Kubla Khan realized that in such a mix, the issue of religion would be crucial. Thus he showed a remarkable openhandedness to all the faiths in his empire. They were all encouraged and supported, so long as they did not threaten the empire. Furthermore, the court frequently heard debates between the different faiths in which different perspectives were presented on pressing moral and social issues. Whilst this cultural mix was the result of the most terrible and dramatic series of conquests by the Mongol hordes, its fruits were a very tolerant society within which great diversity was deliberately encouraged as a sign of high civilization.

A second example comes from India a few centuries later. In the mid to late sixteenth century, a remarkable man ruled much of modern-day India and Pakistan. He was Akbar the Great, a Mogul emperor. He was of course a Muslim, but his tolerance and interest in all the faiths in his domain was remarkable. While Hinduism was not greatly favoured, it was certainly not oppressed during his time. He encouraged debate between Hindus, Muslims and the few Buddhists left in India. He entertained and listened to the beliefs of the Jains and Parsees and invited Christian missionaries based in Goa to his court to discuss Christianity. Here again was a man whose empire had been founded upon bloody conquest by his predecessors, but who out of the cultural and religious mix created a society of tolerance and religious debate.

I find it interesting that in both cases, tolerance and the enjoyment of the diversity of cultures arose after a time of conquest and imperialism. It is not without significance that the rise of intercultural and multicultural interests and societies comes after the period of unparalleled Western colonialism, imperialism and conquest worldwide!

It is also interesting that, while Christians feature in both stories, neither of the stories comes from Christian societies.

The sad fact is that we cannot point to any such figures of tolerance within Christian societies of those times. This is no small matter, for in this sad statement lies a whole history of Christian attitudes towards other faiths and cultures which needs to be looked at briefly before we can understand why Christian societies find pluralism so threatening.

Christianity in its earliest days was but one amongst a number of competing faiths arising from the ferment of the Roman East. It was also the child of two very different systems, both of which, like a child turning on its parents, it was later to attack. The Jewish tradition was soon being despised by the early Christians. St Paul's letters, which compare the Jewish and Christian faiths to the detriment of Judaism, are an early example of the polemical approach to another faith. The unease with the second parent, Greek thought, took longer to emerge, probably because its influence was actually more profound than the Jewish dimension. Yet, within a few years of Christianity's gaining political power in the late Roman empire, the academy at Athens was closed down. Its continued existence, outside the control of the church, was too threatening.

At one level, the history of the early church is a story of success at the expense of other faiths. This has profoundly affected Christian thinking about the nature of diversity in society. Essentially, the Western church was uneasy with diversity in a way which the Eastern church never was. The Eastern church first of all had to exist on the borders of the Christianized Roman world. Syrian Orthodox were as much at home in Antioch, firmly in the Christian empire, as they were in Persia or India. The church of Alexandria had to co-exist (not always comfortably) with a very large Jewish community and with the older traditions of Egypt. With the coming of the Islamic conquests, these churches had to learn to live as part of a state which did not espouse their beliefs, but which did allow them to continue to practise them. Even further east, the Nestorian church in China and Mongolia learned that there was much in the faiths which surrounded them from which they could learn. Indeed, we know that it was through the kind services of a Nestorian priest, Adam, that some of the best translations into Chinese of key Buddhist texts were undertaken.

But none of this happened in the Christianized West. To be sure, older faiths were often absorbed and some indigenous churches such as the Celtic church of Ireland and Scotland took over much from the earlier religions. But what could not be tolerated was the survival of distinct communities. The one exception was the Jews. But they were to become the target of rising intolerance as Christendom began to turn from internal expansion to conquest in the areas of the Islamic empires.

Why? The problem is one of success. The church in India, in China or in Persia, learnt to be a Christian presence, rather than expect to convert the whole of the society it was in. It learned how to witness through their lives and through their actions. It was a presence which often saw much in the surrounding faiths which they could affirm as being godly. In that sense they were indeed like the salt which gives flavour to the meal, or the lamp which lights up the room.

In the West, the situation was very different. With the conversion of the Roman empire to Christianity, and in subsequent centuries, the conversion of many other societies and kingdoms such as the Normans, the Slavs and the Russians, the model was firmly set of total control. The church began to see itself as being able literally to rule the world. It was not enough to have members of the church who lived in a society. You wanted to have the whole society under your command. This accorded well with the profound Greek understanding that at heart there must be one, indivisible unity which supports all, and to which all will return. This deep-seated belief has shaped the response of the West to diversity. It meant that diversity was seen as threatening to this essential unity — essential in the sense that this unity or, to be more correct, this Absolute One — was indeed the very essence of reality. Thus anything which went against this One was seen or felt as profoundly threatening. It explains why the church and Western society were so intolerant not just of other faiths, but especially of other visions of Christianity. This helps us appreciate why heresy was so ruthlessly hunted down and why it was seen not just as a theological problem but also as a social problem. This sense of having to have everything contained in One — be that one church, one faith, one Lord, or within one state under one church — goes some way to explaining why the Western,

Roman church eventually reached what seemed to be the logical conclusion of excommunicating the Eastern, Orthodox church. If reality is One, then there cannot be two sources of authority and two models of the church.

So strong did the identification of "normal" with "Christian" become that when, in later centuries, the West made contact, first with Western Africa and then with America, the church often found it difficult to see those who were not Christian as being really human. While it had a sort of grudging respect for Muslims, who were at least also people of the book, the same respect was not extended to others such as native peoples or indigenous faiths.

There is no doubt that the experience of the near conquest of most of Christendom by the Muslims only helped to further the intolerance and fear of other faiths and cultures. At the time when Kubla Khan was debating with leaders of many different faiths, Christian scholars were translating the Qur'an. However, these translations were not to appreciate Islam better, but the better to attack and denigrate it more effectively.

One might have hoped that the Reformation would have legitimized pluralism, at least within Christianity. Sadly, for complex reasons, it did not. In fact, those churches who spun off from Rome were often even more vehement than Rome itself in insisting that their way was the only possible way. Only with the emergence of the Quakers does a consistent tradition of Christian tolerance and appreciation of other cultures begin to emerge.

The eruption of the mass missionary movement of the Protestant churches during the nineteenth century has already been referred to in the context of the dramatic expansion of church schools. Needless to say, this movement was not sympathetic to diversity. Indeed, it was the most overt attempt by Christianity to remove religious diversity from the face of the earth. Throughout the century and indeed up until the trauma of the first world war, many Christians believed in what John R. Mott so confidently predicted — the evangelization of the world in this generation.

What is so fascinating about this movement is that it chimed in so well with other developments during this century. Take, for example, Darwin's teachings. The traditional picture is of church and science locked into furious debate about the "origins of man". This did indeed happen. The famous debate between the Bishop of Oxford, Samuel Wilberforce, and the scientist T.H. Huxley in 1860 captures that. However, at a popular level, it served to link the idea of evolution and the superiority of Christianity. Both were wedded to the idea of progress and so the theory of evolution could be used to justify the supremacy of Christianity. After all, had not Christian societies become the first industrial, scientific societies? Therefore it must be the case that Europeans were the top of the human evolutionary tree and so Christianity, as their faith, must likewise be the top of the religious tree.

It can be seen in two very different ways that this idea of progress in religion has not yet died out. The Baha'i faith still believes that religion is a steady and logical progression of greater and deeper insights, and charts all the great religious teachers on an upward scale, from Krishna, through Jesus and Muhammad to their prophet Baha'ullah. They believe that as humanity matures, so the need for a more mature message increases and that God, at regular intervals, sends such a messenger. The Baha'is are one of the few groups left for whom the progress and improvement model of human nature and society still holds true.

At a different level, until a couple of years ago, you could still order for use in religious education lessons in the UK a book called *From Fear to Faith*. This book claimed to show how religious belief evolved from the "fearful" religions of "primitive man" and animism, through the polytheistic religions of Hinduism and Buddhism (sic) to the monotheism of Israel and the perfection of faith in Christ. The fact that Islam and Sikhism, to name but two faiths, came after Christianity, did not present a problem. The book just didn't mention them!

The collapse of this evolutionary, world-is-getting-better mentality has caused Christianity no end of problems in its search for a new way of remaining the ultimate and the only one valid way. Two responses have emerged. The first is the Barthian approach, much favoured still by many theologians and educators. This deals with the problem of cultural relativism and the complexities of pluralism and of diverse Christian witness and all the angst of liberal religion by simply denying its worth. By stating that all religion, including "the Christian religion" was "irreligious", it is quite easy to deal with pluralism. A Barthian has no problem studying Buddhism, Islam or Christianity — for they are all interesting, but alas, they are all equally false. Only the direct experience of the breaking in of the word of God could bring true faith. All else is a chimera. Thus all religion stands condemned by the word.

A second approach has emerged in a very different way. I am not even sure that those who espouse it are aware of how exclusive it can be. This is what I would call the "prophetic" church. By that I mean those who have switched their evangelical fervour from converting the world to saving the world — saving it from racism, or poverty, environmental destruction or war. I work a great deal in the area of different faiths and ecology. I sometimes sit squirming with embarrassment while Christians lecture the world on how to care for nature; when clergy tell me that the church must be "prophetic" about our relationship with nature or when church bodies suddenly discover conservation and launch programmes without consultation with any other group. Frankly, the church is a very late comer to ecology. It has little to offer either the secular world or the worlds of different faiths in way of a "prophetic" witness on nature. It needs to recognize that far from having a "prophetic" witness, it has exercised a "pathetic" witness on nature. Yet I watch as church after church — including the World Council of Churches — behave as if Christianity and Christianity alone cares for the world. This pattern of what I call triumphalist morality and social concern is yet another reworking of the model of superiority and of the desire to tell the world what to do. Yes, I know that in many places actual working practice is pluralist — but the language and the structures rarely are.

Nor is this surprising. The Western church as been firmly shaped by an anti-pluralist mentality which it has passed on to those around it. The question therefore becomes, can Christianity handle pluralism in any other way?

It has to. The fact of the matter is that pluralism, religious, ideological, social and economic, is always going to be with us. It has always existed and seems to be an inherent part of our human nature. More than that, it seems to be an inherent *and* essential part of nature per se — of creation. As we deplete the species of the world — by as much as 10,000 species per year — we have come to appreciate the necessity of what is called biological diversity. The fact is that evolution, creation, needs a vast array of difference for life both to continue and to adapt to changing factors. In the mix of biological diversity are species which are very successful; species which are dying out naturally; species which are emerging; species which are parasitical, species which are downright destructive. Yet from this mix comes life, and life anew — so long as we do not reduce this variety, this diversity, to such a low level that there is no possibility of dynamic interaction.

If, as a Christian, I believe that God is the origin of creation, then I must conclude that diversity in creation is part of God's design. Once we can begin to see the necessity of diversity in creation, perhaps we can find it less threatening to consider the necessity of diversity in human belief and action.

That is to say, diversity is not some vast mistake; it is not the result of rebellion against the "known will of God"; it is not a problem which Christianity has to clear up. It is in fact an inherent dimension of being human and of having the God-given resources to draw upon in times of stress and difficulty.

This does not mean that we abandon our critical faculties. So often people assume that to work interculturally, or to be interfaith, one just has to be nice to all, regardless or perhaps precisely because they are different! This is not the case with this model. In recognizing the existence and "usefulness" of diversity — perhaps one could almost say the necessity for diversity — one is not saying that therefore all beliefs are equally valid. To continue the analogy with the rest of nature, some beliefs are helpful to the continuance of life on earth, others are parasitical, others seem to have no particular relevance, others are downright harmful. The skill, or the difficulty, lies in deciding which is which and in being able to defend such a decision.

To affirm diversity to be essential means that we must have both an understanding of the interaction between faiths and cultures and an ability to articulate a higher goal than just the continued existence of diverse beliefs.

If, as Christians, we can come to see diversity as the actual method or means by which God moves us and ensures our

growth, then we can begin to look for
can help us define our relationships with given be-
At present, Christianity is prey to conflicting moods. Because
we cannot see how diversity can be good, we either cut
ourselves off from other influences — or try to — or we opt for
partnership with another belief system which we feel comfortable with. This has been as much the case with right-wing
Christians in the fascist countries of Europe during the 1920s
and 30s as with some in Latin America in their transactions with
Marxism. We need to show a greater ability to be able to
explore and relate to a true diversity.

Let me give an example of the way in which God uses
diversity. Leo Tolstoy, the great nineteenth-century Russian
novelist and Christian, underwent a conversion experience
which radically altered his life. One factor in his conversion,
and in the conversion or religious life of many thousands of
other Russian Christians, was the story of Saint Barlaam and
Saint Josaphat. The main theme of the story concerns a young,
worldly and wealthy prince called Josaphat who meets an other-
worldly monk or hermit called Barlaam. The example of the life
and teachings of this man of God leads Josaphat to be baptized
as a Christian. He then leaves his throne and kingdom and goes
into the wilderness to lead a life of Christian contemplation and
asceticism.

This simple but moving story brought many to an appreciation of Christian truths and a new kind of life-style. But where
does this Russian tale come from? A hint lies in the story, for
the prince is pictured as an Indian ruler who is converted by a
Sinai desert monk — Barlaam. The Russians got the story from
the Greek Orthodox church, who also passed on a version in
Latin to the Western church — reaching Iceland for instance in
an Icelandic translation of 1204 AD.

The Greeks got the story from the Georgians — who were
the first people to convert as a nation to Christianity. The
Georgians had got the story in the seventh to eighth century,
from the Muslims who invaded them! The story is virtually
identical, except that the conversion led to faith in Islam not
Christianity. The Muslims had taken the story from the earlier
central Asian faith of the Manichees. So where did the Manichees get the story from? They got it from the Buddhists of

central Asia — the story is none other than that of the conversion of the Buddha, the wealthy prince Siddhartha Gautama.

The final twist in this story is that when Gandhi wrote, as a young man, to Tolstoy to discuss religion and faith with him, Tolstoy, unaware of the history of the story, recommended it to Gandhi.

Now the issue here is, where does truth lie in all this? The story has functioned as a powerful vehicle of faith, a purveyor of meaning, in a variety of different faiths and to tens of thousands of peoples within those faiths. Yet the story does not really belong to any one of these faiths. Each has found meaning within it. Where exactly lies the truth that is peculiar to any one faith?

Another example would be the image of the mother and child. As Christians we know this as the Virgin Mary and Jesus. Yet many reputable scholars believe Christianity adopted it from the Egyptian cult of Isis and Horus. In turn, Christianity introduced this most powerful of archetypes to the Buddhists of central Asia and western China. There the pair became the goddess of mercy, Kuan Yin, with her child attendant or her gift of a child to barren parents. Again, which is true and by what criteria can we judge this truth?

If this is true of our past, how much more true does this need to be for our future? All religions, all belief systems have a vision of what the individual and the corporate community are part of, and where they are going. Thus the question of what is the vision, the goal, the hopes of religion becomes crucial. This echoes exactly what education has discovered. You can get by for just so long without having to face questions of ultimate meaning and purpose. But eventually, especially in a pluralist society, you have to answer them — or at least acknowledge the need to grapple seriously with them. The challenge to education and to Christianity is, can they now do this in a pluralist way, a way which allows them to retain their integrity while making it possible for them to grow wider than they currently are?

Let us return to the question raised at the beginning of this chapter. Why is it that in the last few decades we have seen society after society, country after country, recognize its multi- or intercultural dimensions? Why is it that the church, with its avowedly anti-interfaith teachings, has had to undergo the traumas of a total reassessment? Why are so many schools today trying to find a way between diverse and at times conflicting value and belief systems, where once they might have been expected to plough a particular furrow, regardless?

The reasons are many. Let us look at a few of them. Every country will have its own specifics, but I hope that at least a few of the following reasons will be relevant in most countries.

In terms of Europe it is probably guilt. The shock of discovering what we could do to minority communities in our midst, which was made plain in the second world war, has deeply affected us. And rightly the horrors of the Nazi death camps for Jews, gypsies, and other groups such as communists and dissident Christians remain with us. It is traumatic to discover that within so many of us lies the possibility of doing such deeds. It is profoundly disturbing to realize the extent to which one's faith and culture have actually prepared the way for such actions. It calls for radical rethinking, the like of which we have not had to do in Europe since the coming of Christianity itself.

It took some years before the logical conclusions could be drawn from the terrible acts of the second world war in Europe. We had to take on board that ordinary "Christian" men and women had either actively taken part in genocide, or had done little to oppose it.

In fairness to the churches, the first real, in-depth thinking took place within them. It was only in the late 1960s that the recognition of diversity in our midst was really taken up by the wider societies. The factor which sparked this and added fuel to the unresolved guilt was the collapse of the old European overseas empires, and immigration. As the European nations such as France, Britain, the Netherlands and Portugal were forced to give up their empires, so we again had to take stock. What on earth had we been dong? By what right? Why had we treated other peoples, cultures and faiths in such extra-ordinary ways? With the realization of what we had done through imperialism and colonization came... yet more guilt. This was further fuelled by the way in which many societies treated the immigrants who were being brought to work in the burgeoning factories of Europe. It was profoundly disturbing to find that we were exhibiting the same signs of racism which had led to the holocaust and which had led us to rule with such insensitivity in our empires. The flag went up. Somehow we had to try and prevent the wheels of history rolling us into yet another pogrom, purge, crusade or holocaust. The answer was seen to lie for the most part in education.

So intercultural education and its twin sister, anti-racist education, were born. But their birth and gradual growth have not been easy. Strongly resisted, they were fragile plants. They also exhibited many of the signs of immaturity. The ideas were half-baked, they often ignored good educational practice and psychology, and they became identified with the left wing of education. Yet, at the same time, they managed to begin some of the most significant work in these areas. They have moved from a situation of facing almost total opposition to being considered an important part of any modern, European expression of values in education. Yet, if truth be told, in many places, only token attention is paid to them, and the values and attitudes taught in subjects which do not seem themselves as being concerned with culture or faith — sciences, maths and geography, for example — frequently undermine the work done in intercultural education.

An interesting example of what happened in one country, West Germany, was given by Herbert Schultze in issue No. 4 of *Interlink*, the magazine of the WCC project on learning in a world of many faiths, cultures and ideologies — a Christian response.

A few months ago I met a young female taxi driver in her mid twenties. She told me about trouble she had experienced in a disco because she argued against a young man who said that Auschwitz never happened. When she insisted that there are still eye-witnesses as well as results of research confirming the facts, some young men of her age beat her up and seriously injured her. Now she was worried because she observed in her environment similar prejudices and violences against Muslims as those against Jews in the past.

Some days ago I went by underground in Hamburg and read on the carriage wall the following graffitti: "Turks kill these pigs by gas"! Not one of the passengers seemed to be disturbed by this horrible inscription.

These observations lead one to question whether there have been sufficient efforts in education to prepare children and young people to meet people of other faiths and cultures. Is there provision to create an atmosphere of mutual understanding?

Schultze then outlines the legal basis for education and especially religious education in the old West Germany. Under the constitution, religious education has to be taught denominationally. This in effect means either Roman Catholic or Protestant (Lutheran). You cannot teach religious education in a Catholic school if you are a Protestant and vica versa.

It was not until the beginning of the 1970s that any syllabuses in Germany started mentioning other faiths than Christianity. Even then, the older missionary approach to other faiths — using them to highlight the superiority of Christianity — was the predominant way in which other faiths found their way into the syllabuses.

Things gradually began to broaden out but, for instance, Judaism began to appear in the history syllabus, mostly concentrating on the Nazi period of 1933 to 1945. Islam appeared under the section on the middle ages and the Turkish advance to the gates of Vienna in 1683. While much of this was inadequate, it opened the doors to discussion and debate and soon the teaching of other faiths was broadened. The rise in numbers of migrants from Turkey working in Germany also acted as a spur to many schools and syllabuses. Some schools celebrated each year the "Day of Foreign Fellow-citizens" while other schools ignored this altogether. The Vatican II declaration on non-Christian religions and positive papers from the German Protestant churches such as "Christians and Jew" and appeals by the churches to welcome Muslim guest workers, had a major impact in opening up the schools and their syllabuses.

Alongside this there was the rise of a call by Muslims for Muslim schools — only one state ever took this up. There is also the increasingly critical examination of text books and syllabuses to ensure that steriotyping and distortion is removed.

Schultze goes on to offer an example of the sort of ways in which the schools have tried to respond to the changing population and cultural groups within their walls.

Just one example of the complex situation behind all these activities may illustrate the problems and opportunities of the teaching of world faiths and different cultures. In the Elsa-Brandstrom School in Frankfurt there are many classes with 90 percent of foreign children... who come from 11 different countries, among others Italy, Morocco, Finland, Brazil, Greece and Lebanon. Their fathers speak a little German at work; their mothers hardly any. Fifteen percent of these children belong to families of doctors, consulate staff, university teachers or students. The other 85 percent live in an area of high crime and prostitution.

The teacher encourages the children to share their ways of life, to tell about celebration of family events, meals or religious festivals. Parents too are invited to tell the class about their home culture.

Some German culture is, like the German language, a major way for the children to communicate. Christian folk festivals like St Martin bring all the children together making lanterns, learning songs and playing instruments. The organization of a school like Elsa-Brandstrom is principally the same as that of schools with only or mostly German children.

Outside of Europe, the many newly emerging nations found they too had to deal with a pluralist society, which had been made more so by immigration policies developed by the old colonial powers. On top of this, they had to work out how to develop a healthy attitude to the remaining white populations. Like the USA, many states assumed that these problems would fade away, could be ignored, or given token attention. Yet the problems have not and will not! An interesting example is Zambia. Here, a mixed population of different indigenous African groupings, white Zambians and Indians have had to try and find a way to live together. Recognizing that the state both needed the support and assistance and the critical involvement of such communities, the Zambian education service has tried to help foster good community relations through education. The religious education syllabus has, certainly since the mid 1960s, tried to reflect and respect the most positive dimensions of each faith and culture. This has tended to mean that what was recommended was rather more "ethical and moral" than religious, but it was an understandable response to this situation. The success of the policy is to be seen in the relative calmness of the intercommunity relationships in that country. In other areas, the vexed issue of history proved an interesting ground for exploring how different groups interpreted the same events in their history. Again, after some shaky starts, good work has emerged here, in many ways better in terms of recognizing how subjective history can be than many European syllabuses.

In the other ex-colonies, places such as the USA, Canada, Australia and so forth, the experience was different yet again. In all these countries, the basic assumption until the late 1960s was that the vast array of different cultures and faiths were to be subordinated and eventually absorbed by "white" values, and by the principles of self-help and independence. The discovery that this was not working took some time to sink in. In the USA, it needed law cases, riots and the civil rights marches to bring this home. Even then, there was strong resistance to exploring the differences inherent in the states. An even more recent arrival on the intercultural scene is Australia, where the very controversial issue of the Aborigines still causes major problems. To fully appreciate what has happened to these peoples, one needs to re-examine whole areas of the curriculum, such as history and geography. Again, it has only been through the stridency of a few that the need to recognize diversity and to learn how to handle it has arisen.

And this is the key to why intercultural, interfaith education has had such a tough time; why it is seen, rightly, as being so threatening, and why it is so essential. For at the heart of intercultural education is the question of how do groups with at times totally divergent views live together? For some, intercultural education or interfaith activities in general should concentrate only on what unites. For others it is important to explore what makes us distinctive, to learn skills for living with, exploring and appreciating this difference. One is essentially the old, let's-all-be-one mentality, which while it seems to accept pluralism, actually finds it very worrying. The other accepts diversity as essential to human life and society, and seeks to find ways to understand its dynamic role.

But what does this all mean for actual education today, and for the Christians, the churches and the children caught up in these momentous times?

4. Can We Have Diversity in Education?

There is no doubt that diversity of beliefs, values and ideologies within a society can wreck it. Take India as an example, a society which has traditionally, for the last four hundred years or so, exhibited considerable ability in handling diversity. Home to four major faiths, Hinduism, Buddhism, Jainism and Sikhism, it has also been invaded by and accommodated Islam, and Christianity since at least the fourth century if not earlier. For the last five or six hundred years it has offered a home to fleeing Zoroastrians who have become the Parsees, and has spawned countless smaller religious groups.

When India emerged as an independent country after a long struggle, it lost much of its Islamic lands and peoples. The distress and bloodshed of that division led the founders of the state to conclude that only an avowedly secular state could handle the pluralism that existed. Religion was to be relegated to the private lives of individuals and not allowed to influence the public domain. In following this path, the leaders saw themselves as drawing upon the best of conventional thinking, namely Western secular philosophy about the state, and as having neatly solved the issue of religion. Education followed this line, including the church schools which, as we saw, had been set up with the explicit purpose of propagating the Christian way against others.

The experiment has to a great extent failed. India is now riven with religious and cultural strife: Sikh against Hindu; Hindu against Muslim. Tribal peoples and those outside the caste system soon discovered that the secular Indian state had no space for them, unless they conformed to the norms of the majority culture.

In the Soviet Union, religious and cultural diversity was seen as something which would wither away under the bright sunshine of the socialist state. Apart from the odd dance, folk costume and song, diversity was suppressed. What is happening now is that these suppressed differences are tearing the old Soviet "empire" apart. Here again, education saw its role as preparing peoples of all cultures to be citizens of the state, speaking, acting and believing the same way. Education failed, and ten years before the present changes, teachers were asking for help with religious and cultural diversity, whilst still officially maintaining that these did not, or should not, matter.

So what are we to do with diversity?

I believe that education has to grasp the issue firmly and accept diversity. I believe that the church needs to accept and learn to see God's hand in diversity. I believe that we need to start facing up to the fact that, for better or for worse, diverse patterns of behaviour, of beliefs and of values will always be with us.

What I do not believe is that we really gain anything by "lowest common denominator" programmes. By this I mean, find areas where, by suppressing our differences, we can find a superficial agreement or even unity. I believe that we should look at the things that divide us, at the different goals and aspirations we have, and at the different points of origin.

I do not believe that discovering that we all consider peace to be a good idea is of the slightest help. That most Buddhists, Christians, Muslims, Hindus or what have you think that peace is a good idea hasn't helped much. What we need to do is find what it is that irritates, upsets or radicalizes the believers; what it is that makes them feel comfortable or uncomfortable. What we really need to do is to find ways of conflict resolution which appeal to or build upon traditions within each faith and culture. We need to find ways of handling what actually exists. In this way, our diversity may itself actually offer us different models of conflict resolution and help us evolve yet newer ones for situations which our forebears never experienced.

So what does this mean for education? It means that education has to start by accepting diversity as extant, as legitimate and as significant. But how?

Let us look at two examples, both of which I have been involved in in one way or another. The first is not taken from state or formal education. It is taken from a rather unlikely source — Christian nurture material. It has been traditional in Christian nurture material — such as the material used in Sunday schools and confirmation classes and for catechism — for the existence of other values and beliefs to be either totally ignored, or to be used to give Christians a sense of superiority. This is done by citing a practice or belief in another faith and then comparing it unfavourably with the way Christians behave. The classic victims of this practice are the Jews, followed by the Muslims. This has done immense damage to the ability of

...g Christians to relate to friends and colleagues of other faiths.

The National Council of Churches of Kenya, in association with the WCC Interlink project, set out to try and develop a model for teaching which would, from a Christian perspective, accept, celebrate and seek to understand pluralism in society. The book opens with a spread of pictures showing different faiths in Kenya at worship. From this introduction of diversity, the book tries to explore the tensions and the possibilities of being a committed Christian in the midst of diversity. Its purpose is clearly stated: "These pages affirm that we accept, as part of reality, different and diverse ways of believing. We are not afraid of this, for it is what we all experience. What we need to do is make some sense of it."

The course then looks at fundamental beliefs about God and about being human beings, and draws upon insights within other faiths, and especially from traditional African religions, which help illuminate the Christian path as being both distinctive and as having something to learn from other understandings.

The intention of the course is simple. It is to help young Christians feel proud of being Christians, but not at the expense of being able to live and interact in a society which is very pluralist.

The second example is from the world of formal education. The most widely translated and distributed interfaith text book in Europe is a book and teacher's notes called *Worlds of Difference*. The book, of which I was a co-author, came out of a project involving many faith organizations and environmental groups around the world. First published in Britain in 1985, it has now been translated into six European languages and gone through many reprints. Yet when it first came out it was attacked vigorously. What disturbed many was its title and the assumption behind it. The norm in interfaith books for schools to that date was that we were all part of one world and that we needed to realize this. This book was saying that we may live in one physical world, but we actually see, experience and relate to radically different worlds. Hence the title, "Worlds of Difference".

The subject matter of the book is the different ways in which various belief systems (the book covers a range from Australian Aboriginal, Chinese folk religion, Christianity and Hinduism through to the Yoruba of Nigeria, taking in humanism en route) view the natural world in the light of their beliefs about its origin and meaning, and what this means in terms of their treatment of the environment. The basic premise of the book and its support materials (wall-charts, TV and radio programmes) is that the very different ways certain societies and faiths treat the natural world are rooted in what their foundational beliefs — creation stories — tell them about its significance and the place of human beings within the system.

The writers make it very clear why they see this diversity as being important. Firstly, they make the point that if we are to survive the environmental crisis, we need to radically re-examine our beliefs about the world, which have brought so many of us to abuse it. Secondly, many faiths and belief systems have values and attitudes which show us a more caring attitude to nature — attitudes which we may need to explore further if we are to reform our own cultures. Thirdly, they make it very apparent that they do not believe any one faith or belief system is capable of helping us solve the environmental crisis by itself. What is needed is a dynamic interaction between what at times appear to be diametrically opposed visions of what nature means and what role human beings have within it. Only from such an interaction, the authors argue, can any new models and ideas emerge.

The results of this book have been dramatic. Having opened up the idea of learning from and within the different faiths and cultures about nature, the World Wide Fund for Nature International, the world's largest environmental charity, decided to invite all the faiths to Assisi in Italy in 1986, to meet with the main environmental organizations. The Network on Conservation and Religion has developed from this with over 80,000 religious communities from eight world religions worldwide now engaged in ecology. It seeks to help faiths develop their own, and where appropriate interfaith, pro-grammes on ecology.

By celebrating diversity and by seeing it as a resource which is vitally needed today, the book offers a dynamic picture of pluralism as not just something which exists, not just something which could be of interest, but as something which we actually need in order to survive.

Now, in both cases, the Kenyan Christian nurture scheme and the "Worlds of Difference", the schemes had clear, higher goals than simply the study of diversity. In other words, they had goals which helped both to make sense of and to give meaning to the existence of and study of diverse traditions. As we have seen earlier, it is this greater goal which education needs to have if it is to do justice to diversity. But how can education have such a goal if the society does not support it? And what goal or goals can it have in a situation of diversity, often indeed of division between peoples?

As we commented earlier, education always has to be seen as being value-laden. The values must arise from the society, even if they are not the actual majority values of the society. However, if the values espoused by education are too far removed from what the bulk of society, or the power forces in society, believe are important, then education will find itself cut off and starved of resources, respect and ultimately of power.

In many societies today, pluralism is given a nod of respectability. This is often more out of a sense of necessity than out of conviction. It often seems as if governments are only too aware of the potential for dissent within pluralism, and so try to use intercultural education as one means of control. At one level this is fair enough. No one wants intercommunal violence or aggression. It is perfectly legitimate for governments to seek to develop a shared sense of purpose. The tension comes if this runs counter to deeply held beliefs, or is propagated at the expense of such beliefs. Not that any state can ever afford to allow equal status to all beliefs. In a pluralist society, overtly racist groups, religious or ideological, have to be controlled for the sake of the wider good.

An interesting example of a state trying to handle diversity within the context of overall societal needs as they are perceived, is Singapore. In an article in *Interlink* No. 2, the editors drew upon a paper by Prof. Ong Jin Hui presented at the conference on the Asia-Pacific culture, its history and prospects, in Tenri, Japan, which outlined what the government was doing.

> In 1979, the ministry of education announced that it was implementing a new programme for all Singapore school children which would provide them with the moral basis for life in an

increasingly complex society. This was followed by an announce-
ment in 1982 that religious knowledge would be a compulsory
subject by the beginning of the 1984 school year. Stated baldly, it
did not seem to be as significant or as difficult a task as it turned
out to be.

The programme of moral education and religious studies to be
implemented by the ministry of education did not, of course,
spring full-grown into reality. As in many other innovations in
Singapore's educational programme, many questions were raised,
and agonized over, before the programme came into being.

Given the sensitive nature of the subject and the multi-racial,
multi-religious, multi-lingual and multi-cultural context in which it
evolved, the challenge of getting the programme started must have
seemed almost as daunting as the problems it was designed to
resolve.

The basic assumptions and factors leading to the government
focussing on this problem were quite clearly spelt out in the
expressions of concern made by various ministers and officials of
the ministry of education, but essentially they centred on the
following elements:

"The main aims of education are to strengthen moral and civic
education and to raise the effectiveness of the education system.

This means we have to improve the teaching and the learning
of language and raise the standards of technical education.

Moral and civic education is mainly taught through the subject
Education for Living (a combination of civics, history and geography) in the pupil's mother tongue. Its aim is to teach social
discipline and national identity and to imbue in pupils moral and
civic values.

While pupils will learn and acquire more and more knowledge
of science and Western technology and be proficient in the English
language, they will be taught not to adopt the life-styles and values
of the West that are alien and pernicious to Singapore society."
(*The Straits Times*, 13 February 1977 — Addendum to the Pres-
idential Address)

Later in the year, the following statement was made:

"Working parents, who spend less and less time with their
children, have had to depend more on the school to provide moral
guidance and training.

The school, on the other hand, had to reckon with the increasing pressure exerted by society on its purpose and functions, and
while proper teaching of certain subjects involved a certain amount
of morality, the main stress was invariably academic and intellectual.

Young people today are growing up in an age of religious scepticism, moral confusion and almost universal uncertainty because of the questioning of traditional values and beliefs.

To an earnest young person, it must sometimes seem that there is no longer a generally accepted moral code and a set of standards for behaviour which everyone is able to quote and subscribe to with confidence." (*The Straits Times*, 10 July 1977 — Mr Chai Chong Yi, minister of state for education)

Here is a classic study on what a state wants from intercultural, interfaith education. It has a clear set of values which it wants passed on to its young, and a clear idea of what forces are threatening it. The question arises, of course, what if some of the questioning and scepticism commented upon is really necessary? An example, not to do with Singapore specifically, is that most majority cultures and faiths have been historically sexist. Do we wish them to continue to be sexist? If we do not, then we need to look for a critical engagement, not just a docile acceptance of what has always been.

Japan offers a fascinating view on all this. There what education is about is not controversial. Japan does not see itself as a pluralist society — hence the great difficulty it has with its own indigenous peoples and with communities such as the Koreans. As Roger Goodman of the Nissan Institute of Japanese Studies, Oxford, said in an article in *Interlink* No. 2:

Japan has built its modern progress around the assumption of being a homogeneous, one-culture nation. Economic prosperity and freedom from the crime rates characteristic of Western countries are commonly explained as due to this sense of sharing a common tradition... The problem for the Japanese "establishment" is how to encourage this sense of a common culture and tradition and at the same time continue to compete so successfully in the world.....

One issue that has drawn attention to this concern is what to do with Japanese children who have been exposed to a pluralist society by living away from Japan. These children, usually of business people or diplomats, have attended international schools and thus rubbed up against all sorts of different beliefs, values and groups. The Japanese government response is to see them as in some way contaminated. As Goodman goes on to say in his article:

...there seems to be widespread agreement (or perhaps the unquestioning assumption) that "kikokushijo" [a term used to describe returnee children] suffer not only academically but also culturally on their return to Japan. These cultural problems are thought to stem from the fact that Japan is a homogeneous, exclusivist, group-oriented society with an "island mentality" compounded by two centuries of isolation, where human relations are based on ideas of harmonious consensus, whereas many "kikokushijo" are believed to be coming back from open, pluralistic societies where the notion of the individual is stressed.

The result is that many such children undergo de-programming designed to rid them of the subversive ideas and values they have picked up. Well, that is one approach to intercultural education.

The need for a clear goal need not take us into the extremes of Japan, nor into the anti-change ideas implicit in the Singapore model. As stated earlier, I believe that education has to have a goal or goals by which it judges its worthwhileness. These goals will, of necessity, reflect aspects of contemporary society, but will also be seeking to build towards a better society. It is common in the West to assume that the child and the child alone is the goal of education. This is an illusion, for the child does not exist in a vacuum, but as part of a society. Nor is education a goal in itself. Thus I return to the question: how do we find such a goal and a sense of direction?

The Dutch education system is one of the most thoroughly officially intercultural in the world. Intercultural education work has been going on in the Netherlands for nearly twenty years, and the Dutch can congratulate themselves on some fine official stances and policies. However, there seems to be a growing crisis in the gap between policy and practice, not least in the area of religious education and associated studies.

One of the specific projects run by the Interlink project for the WCC was a study of the Dutch interfaith educational system. The results raised many issues of how interfaith education can be done. Essentially, we asked our Dutch colleagues to study religious education and intercultural studies in Dutch Christian schools. We asked them not to look at what was taught, but why it was taught. To what end was interfaith and cultural education being taught in schools which were avowedly

Christian? The Dutch system allows different belief systems to run schools, which the state supports financially.

In 1989 the Dutch team reported back on their work, beginning with a pertinent observation and question:

> ...the question "To what end are Christian teachers and Christian schools involved in intercultural religious education?" seemed to be inadequately formulated. It should be better to formulate this question as follows: "To what end are Christian teachers and Christians schools involved in educating all children?" However, no clear answer was found to the question. In fact we found that all education has been aimed at cognitive uniformity: Western, scientifically positivistic. (Page 4 of the final *Interlink*)

The researchers identified a set of six major categories of factors that hinder effective intercultural education which by law these schools are supposed and are indeed deemed to be delivering.

1. *The stalemate situation within the schools:* Educational features of these situations are:
— conflicting views among the staff, related to educational aims, means and (religious) attitudes;
— conflicting views between director/teachers and school board, related to educational aims and means;
— conflicting views between school and parents of indigenous pupils, referring to social and/or religious expectation;
— conflicting views within the teachers' minds, referring to tension between their personal beliefs as Christians and their professional roles as teachers; a feeling of being left in the lurch by their local churches.

2. *Willingness to cooperate with teachers who have different opinions:* Tutors of Christian schools find it difficult to agree on a common view of the role of religions in a pluriform school...

3. *The traditional theological background:* The theological background of religious education is mainly traditional; the subject is taught from a model by which (implicitly) revelation has already happened and salvation has been given. The unchangeable God rules history which — with disregard to the present — discloses the future as a perfect history. But is the present not a bridge to the future? Logically as well as theologically?

4. *The educational consequences of the religious view of human nature:* Many teachers have no explicit, clear, theological vision of other religions. Implicitly the current vision covers either

the idea of the analogia entis [analogy of being] or the idea of the analogia fidei [analogy of faith]....

5. *The dominance of the Western cognitive uniformity:* ... Scientific positivism pretends to release humanity from the slavery of myths, but in neglecting the inability of such an approach to cope with phenomena which cannot be quantified, and ignoring the fact that society reflects and creates the structure of knowledge, have we in the West not been guilty of making scientific positivism into a new religion, a new mythology?

6. *The dominance of prescriptive dogmatics:* As long as practice is seen as secondary in importance in endorsing religious truth, the chance of a revision of Christian principles will be minimal. Nevertheless with a view to the child's personal development it seems to be necessary to gain a new harmony between principles and practice especially in relation to religious development. Can schools articulate an aim for religious education which is not just that of being an extension of either the church or the family?

The answer to many of these concerns, the Dutch team concluded, lay in a new theological model and a new definition of the goal of education and of the church. To this end they have mooted the image of the kingdom of God on earth. They see this term as embracing the affirmation of the divine but within the context of the day-to-day lives of ordinary people. They see the kingdom as being an open place, where difference is seen as part of the gifts each people brings to the greater vision and community of the kingdom. They also feel it offers both the church and education a goal which has realizable aspects for the here and now, but with a greater goal in the future.

The Dutch "kingdom of God" model is attractive, but others in the Interlink team felt that this notion immediately raised questions of language and meaning. It may work for Christians, but what does it mean to an atheist or a Buddhist? Can we simply absorb them into our bigger vision, without so much as a by-your-leave?

I think, in fairness, that the Dutch team was looking for a vision which could at least bring Christians in education, the church in education and theology into an active relationship with pluralism. As such it merits further work. I also think that in many ways, the work which is being done exploring differences as providing models to help solve or cope with social, economic or political crises are in fact positing that there is a greater goal of social wellbeing — the kingdom of God — which gives direction and meaning to the evaluation and understanding of different belief stances. In other words, if we look to see what different faiths have to offer to economic alternatives, we are positing that just economics is worth striving for — an aspect of the kingdom.

Diversity is here to stay. Education and each distinct belief system must discover some model for understanding and interpreting this fact. Currently, as we have seen, there are many ways in which people and systems are trying to handle this fact. Education is seeking to discover its special role, while also struggling with its need for a goal. There are interesting and encouraging signs from around the world. But there are also signs that the basic human need for security is being profoundly threatened by pluralism and can cause education to either revert to older, trusted models which exclude difference, or to using difference as a means of social control and power. In the Dutch example we see how good intentions are not enough. These have to be backed by reappraisal and a new definition of purpose both within education and within support groups such as the church. The question of ends and means, of goals for the child, for the school, for the community and for the society, becomes crucial.

It is this that we must look at in greater detail — the fundamental question of goals and the means for achieving these goals.

5. So What Do We Do?

In this final chapter, I want to look at the role of "objectivity" in education, for this fundamentally affects the perception of whether education can have any societal or value goals. I want to suggest three basic steps Christians can use to help develop and analyze new ways of education and new ways for Christians to be partners in education. Finally, I want to tell a story, one which we think we know, but which may have a slightly different ending from the one we imagine. I hope that through the ideas given here, Christians can begin to reassess what it means to be educators and to be involved in formal education. So let me start with what is really rather an important question.

Does contemporary, standard, Western-oriented education have a goal? In many national cases one would have to answer, officially, no. But the reality is very different. The reality was hinted at in the six points made in the Dutch report, as we saw in the last chapter. The reality is that such education is geared towards producing compliant members of a world-view which is best summarized as the reductionist, consumer model. In other words, education, as currently experienced, especially in the majority world, is espousing values and a goal — consumer-oriented society — which actually runs counter to much within both religious and ideological world-views.

At the World Council of Churches' conference on "Faith, Science and the Future", held at the Massachusetts Institute of Technology, Cambridge, USA, in 1979, Prof. Mahinda Palihawadana from Sri Lanka expressed his perception of what was the implicit goal and values of Western education thus:

> How science has affected the religious quality of Buddhist communities is a many-sided question. What is most obvious may be stated first: more than science itself, more than the inner nature of its methodology and its logic, it is the creeping materialism of new life-styles that has been cutting into both the visible cultural fabric and even the intangible spiritual content of the Buddhist's religiousness.

What does this actually mean in practice? The Interlink project had a team working primarily in the Philippines on the issues of the role of values, diversity and science and technology education. The team looked at contemporary school textbooks used to teach science to grades 4 and 5, to see to what extent the books explicitly taught science as a value-laden topic, or presented it as value-free, whilst actually advocating a particular set of values.

Their conclusions were more disturbing than we had expected and led to questions in the Philippines parliament and statements by government officials. It also attracted considerable attention from the media under headlines such as "Textbooks teach tots wrong ideas about environment". The report showed that the textbooks currently in use (though they have now been withdrawn) were operating on a dominant model basis. As it illustrated, there are profoundly disturbing forces at work, forces which those of us brought up in the system often fail to see.

This model [the dominant model] operates on two basic levels:

— It assumes that there is one and only one model of science and technology. And this is the "dominant model". It implicitly says that all other models are either myth or superstition. A "scientific way of thinking" is contrasted with fables and what are implied to be primitive and backward ideas without explaining their context or the different "ways of thinking and living" that may have produced them. These other ways of thinking and living are largely brushed aside as "unscientific" because they do not conform to, or even conflict with, the dominant model.

— While it emphasizes systems, the "dominant model" isolates the parts of the system. Interactions and relations are oversimplified to explain "laws" in a very mechanical manner. In this sense, the dominant model is called reductionist. Cause-and-effect relationships are purely physical and short-term, not social and historical. The "history of science" is presented as a simple series of "discoveries", with their cultural causes and effects rarely being tackled. The model also propagates a consumerist, Western-oriented view of the world. People are not only separated from nature, they are supposed to exploit nature. Scientific "discoveries" are more often than not attributed to scientists from the West as if the East had no role in the development of science.

The report then looked at the role of reductionism in the books. The researchers pointed out that a basic tendency within reductionist thinking is to reduce relationships to oversimplistic statements. For example, they cite the grade 5 textbook where four lessons are devoted to separating and classifying aspects of nature; this assumes that these relationships are the most important ones in the relationships of these beings. Thus the classifications are such simplistic groupings as "animals with backbones", "animals without backbones" and "plant groups".

The researchers noted that there was no attempt to show that flora and fauna are part of a vast complex eco-system — a system in which we too have a place, and not just as observer and classifier. The lack of examination of the inter-relationships meant that children were not being taught to see the fragile and vulnerable nature of the eco-system or the damaging role of human beings. This becomes even more acute when the consumerist viewpoint is then brought to bear on it. Let the researchers' report spell out what they mean:

> Many examples on the element of consumerism run parallel with those on reductionism. Consumerist attitudes may be developed by the "food links" framework discussed earlier in this section. Only consumption relationships are shown in such linkages. This may imply that only such relations matter.
>
> In the grade 5 book, within the lessons on plant and animal classification, species are further classified only according to their usefulness. The following excerpt speaks for itself:
>
> "Reptiles are also useful animals. Some are used for food by man. Monitor lizards are hunted for their meat in some places. Turtle's meat and eggs are as delicious as those of a chicken. The skin of snakes and crocodiles is made into leather. This kind of leather is expensive. Leather out of crocodile skin measuring 2½ square cm costs about one peso."
>
> (Illustrations of bags, shoes, and belts made of crocodile leather are also shown.)
>
> Later, the lesson attempts to save itself by saying:
>
> "Crocodiles and turtles are constantly hunted by people. If this is not stopped, they will soon disappear from our country. We do not want this to happen. What can you do to help?"
>
> The same usefulness criterion is applied to mammals, shells and insects. After the child is repeatedly bombarded with such a framework it will not be surprising if he or she can only offer a perplexed stare when asked what pupils "can do to help". (*Interlink* final report)

It is obvious, therefore, that Western education carries with it the seeds of a world-view which is profoundly disturbing. In particular, science and technology, with its claims to be value-free, poses a threat. Ironically, whilst science should be the most self-critical of disciplines, it has actually become and been experienced, especially in the majority world, as an inflexible bearer of Western, reductionist and consumer values. These run counter to what many feel are the values most needed in our world today.

Yet, so often, standard education sees itself as being objective and value-free. The Singapore government has a case, at one level, when it sees the dangers in Western attitudes and values. Where it is wrong is in trying to prevent change and adaptation. The Philippines team had a vision of what education should be doing and the values which it should be espousing. This they found not only missing in the contemporary materials in schools, but actually being undermined by the values which the books present. They want a dynamic relationship between the present situation and the vast changes occurring in their society. The Singapore government, on the other hand, seems to have a set of values which it wishes to preserve against the corroding influences of the West and this seems to lead to a model where engagement and change are not encouraged. And this is a problem. Nothing stands still. Faiths survive by adapting and responding, not by shutting out differences. They survive because they are able to assess the validity of changes by the criteria of their core beliefs, values and goals. Religions on the whole are able to recognize themselves as vehicles of values and beliefs. Sadly, science and technology have not yet recognized the extent to which they do exactly the same. The desire to appear "objective" is still a strong motivating belief in science which is used to legitimate the role and function — and often the power — of science and technology. But it is an illusion.

Education seems to share this desire for the Holy Grail of "objectivity". Much of secular, formal, state education seeks to hide behind the notion of objectivity, as if this were possible and as if this then meant that you were value-free. Even state religious education in certain countries has fallen into this trap of an objective, value-free ideal. Take for instance religious education in the UK. The rise of interfaith religious education took place at a time when the phenomenological approach to it was most fashionable. This meant that religious education saw itself as simply studying "facts" about faiths: what different religious buildings look like; what different religious leaders are called; what festivals are celebrated by different religions. Rarely if ever did it ask questions of why. That would be to lose the "objectiveness" of the phenomenological approach. Religious education saw itself as just reporting on what was. Yet the very fact that religious education was now interfaith meant changes in the faiths' own perspectives. An example might help to illustrate what I mean.

Soon after interfaith religious education began, the Muslims successfully persuaded educational publishers that in any books on Islam or sections of books where Islam was dealt with, the Islamic injunction against images should be adhered to. In the past this has been fairly loosely adhered to. There are plenty of Islamic pictures of animals, people, even of angels. But nowadays, the norm is to adhere to the Qur'an and to prohibit any representation of living things, and most especially of the Prophet Muhammad or any of the angels, the other prophets or God. So, no pictures of Allah, angels, Muhammad and so forth. This immediately meant that the books themselves were accepting and emphasizing the beliefs and values of one faith. But more was to come from this. The Sikhs have been split over the last few years by the rise of the Khalistani movement. This movement seeks an independent Sikh state. Its great hero is the last guru of Sikhism, Guru Gobind Singh. He has become elevated to an almost divine position. A book claiming to contain his ninety-nine prophecies foretells the creation of such a state in the very near future. As part of the campaign to give Guru Gobind Singh a new status, above and beyond that of the other nine gurus, some Sikhs have started to demand that publishers do not put pictures of him in the sections on Sikhism — in just the same way as the Muslims argued earlier. This has presented educational publishing with a dilemma. Whilst it is clear that all of contemporary Islam follows the Qur'anic ruling against images, it is not clear what the authority basis is for the Sikh claim. Thus religious education, by its very fact of being interfaith, comes to involve religious-political dimensions which means it is part of new forces shaping Sikh self-perception. In its resolution of this struggle over images, it will add weight to one side or another in this inter-Sikh debate. Where is objectivity in such a case?

As I have said earlier, education is never value-free, least of all when it thinks it is! Thus, in planning and hoping for a livable pluralist world, we need to look very carefully at the values which any education system does have. These values will be determined, at least in part, by the goals. But what are the goals which a pluralist society can have? What in particular is the role and place of Christians and Christian goals and values in such an educational system?

I believe that there are three steps which Christians in education and the church in education have to take in order to be able to play a helpful role in this process. By implication, much of what I am about to say also applies to education per se, from whatever viewpoint one comes at it. All aspects of education are carriers of values and world-views. All need to see to what extent their values, beliefs and world-views need to be changed by the challenge of pluralism and the question of goals and means to goals. As we discovered when working with the International Association for Intercultural Education — a secular worldwide agency for intercultural education studies — we are quite happy to talk about all aspects of the curriculum becoming pluralist, but not the actual pluralization of education. When did you last hear anyone talking about intercultural education! It is a significant omission.

So what are these three steps for Christians in education?

The first is theological. Until we have a new model and understanding of diversity, we cannot make any progress. No amount of tinkering with our current ideas will help — for they all seem to function on the basis of trying to reconcile or find a place for the other faiths within Christianity. The inherent Christian fear or suspicion of diversity has to go and be replaced by an acceptance that God works through diversity and diversity therefore is part of the way of God on earth. As we have stressed earlier, this does not mean an uncritical acceptance of all diverse forms. Far from it. It actually calls for some major reassessments of not just the role and place of other faiths and belief structures, but also of considerable sections of Christian teaching and practice. In the past, Israel or the church looked to the prophets such as Amos and Hosea or great reforming saints such as Bernard or Francis for this critique, this agenda of issues which helped us evaluate the contribution of contemporary faith. Now, I would argue, it is increasingly the "secular" world which offers or challenges us with these criteria.

To achieve this, we need to go right to the heart of our own teaching. The Kenyan scheme for pluralistic Christian nurture only touches the tip of an iceberg. Statements from bodies such as the WCC are fine on issues like dialogue, but what we really need is to re-examine and redesign the way we nurture people and ourselves in the faith. At present too much of the sense of Christian identity is created by either ignoring the rest of the world's values and belief systems and acting as if only Christians were right or caring or concerned with justice and so on, or by scoring points off other faiths in order to bolster our own sense of superiority. In the very way we portray what it means to be Christian, we need to see that as being within a context of greater diversity and variety. This means that the real area for the churches to explore the consequences of interfaith dialogue is in Sunday school syllabuses, confirmation classes and catechetics. To realize this, we need to know why diversity is here and what to make of it.

Once the churches have begun this job, we can then hope that Christians will reflect in their everyday thoughts and actions a critically positive attitude towards diversity.

But to have a critically positive attitude we need goals in the light of which we can assess the role and significance of different faiths and belief systems, including Christianity.

The second step is concerned with goals which are appropriate and viable for a pluralist society and with the integrity of the means developed or used to strive for such goals. Within this, education's role is to aid in the discernment of such goals, to assist in promoting appropriate methods and to ensure the fostering and advancement of these ideas.

But what exactly can we have as goals of such a society? Perhaps we have already seen some of them emerging in the earlier chapters. One goal is to have a sustainable, integrated environment. That is a goal worth having and one which, if we do not work for it, will mean there will be no human race to worry about anyway! If such a world-view — a sustainable, inter-related environment in which humanity is a part, but only a part — were to be a goal of society, then it is clear what role education can play in it. It can start by abandoning all that makes for a reductionist, materialist and consumer-driven world-view over against a holistic one; it can stop viewing the natural world in terms of utilitarian, anthropocentric models of meaning; it can start assessing economics, industry, life-styles, history, etc. in the light of the role they have to play in either ensuring such a world-view, or in having done much to undermine it. In the sphere of religion, it will mean education looking at the different ways in which faiths have treated the natural world and at the different ways they understand it and our role in nature. This will almost certainly mean that the movements within Christianity to rid our faith of its environmentally destructive attitudes will proceed apace. In other words, Christians will probably discover that in the midst of diverse views about nature, it is our faith that needs to be seen as one of the potentially most dangerous and greatly in need of reform, but also as one with a potential for a constructive contribution which has been smothered by traditional understandings which we can now remove in order to rediscover the faith's original vision.

Another goal should be the resolution of conflict and the quest for justice in and through such resolution. Diversity by its very nature is not peaceful, but it only becomes divisive if people try to force diverse ways into one way. So, conflict-resolution becomes both a means and in part, at least, a goal along with the search for justice. This means looking at the way in which education itself deals with tensions within itself. The Dutch project report quoted in chapter 4 saw the internal conflicts within actual schools to be a major area of concern which would require patient attention if any seriously developmental education is to take place. On a wider scale, the need to be able to resolve conflicts is crucial for a world of accepted diversity. Education's role in studying different ways and means of achieving conflict-resolution is vital. History, religious and cultural traditions, science, philosophy, law, art — all these can teach us potential models of conflict-resolution as well as examples of the breakdown of groups and communities. Out of these we can begin to fashion means and ends appropriate for today. The role of justice in all of this is that of an indicator of the fairness and equality of any model of conflict-resolution. If justice is not served by these models, then they are not the models which should be pursued.

Creativity is another goal. So much of our emphasis in education stresses knowledge along the lines of the two-books idea — Word and Nature as knowledge. Education on the whole still views creativity as suspect, unless it is in the area of creative writing. Many have commented, looking at the ancient carvings and religious sites of, for instances, medieval Europe or Vedic India, what a large percentage of the population must have been skilled craftsfolk to have created and sustained so many fine works of art. We have lost much of this creativity. An educational system which valued creativity would make possible a society in which creativity was not just possible but normal. How many people have you come across who wish they could paint, draw, sing, dance, play a musical instrument?

It is also important for education and, if possible, for society, to have a built-in acceptance of shortcomings! In other words, we know we shall never develop the perfect system of education, so we must ensure that built into such systems are the facilities, the skills and the possibilities for critical self-assessment or for critical assessment by others. This requires maturity and, ironically, much more confidence than those systems which appear to know what they are doing and do not set out to provide such opportunities. The need for what one might call the Socrates factor is only too clear as we watch the systems of Eastern Europe and of the old USSR crumble — systems which brooked no criticism and had no ability to self-criticize.

Some people might want to call such goals signs of the kingdom. Well, maybe. I am not sure. I believe we need to be very careful about telling people this is what God wants. I think we should do what is right for all creation and what we feel is right for all of us, and trust that God will bless it. As soon as we start to hoist theological terms on to goals, we run the risk of discovering that they are not appropriate or workable, but we are then stuck with them. For just as we have to accept the diversity of society, so we shall have to work out a way of handling the diversity of goals. This presents formidable political difficulties, and as Christians we can only try to see if, within our own faith community, we can handle differences, and these experiences may then have something to offer to the wider society. The ecumenical process, faltering, botched, heroic, foolish and noble as it is, is perhaps one of the most important models that the church has to offer to the wider world, of what to do and what not to do in handling diversity. The criteria by which we make decisions of the worthwhileness of goals is in part explored in step three. However, the experience of the ecumenical movement seems to indicate that while one set of criteria may set you off in pursuit of a given goal, the journey towards that goal will profoundly affect the criteria. Taking the ecumenical movement, the original criterion was the scandal of the divisions in the mission field, meaning a divided witness to the heathen. Then the criteria became one of returning to an organic unity spoken of by Jesus in St John's Gospel. Later still, it was seen as the churches' contribution to the One-World idea. Now, many would see it as being an attempt to hold in creative tension the diversity of Christian expression, without the divisions which have so marred the history of Christianity. Criteria and goals have a dynamic relationship!

Finally we come to the third step — the integrity of intention. Let me give a classic example of what I mean. A major international conservation body receives a report which shows that aircraft do immense damage to the ozone layer and fuel the greenhouse effect. So they decide they must cut down on their own international air travel, so as to set an example and to help reduce the global amount of air travel. They launch a major two-year study project in which the biggest item is air travel...! This is a true story.

In looking at intentions, we need to be able to see clearly the goals to which they are a pathway. This is why the second step in these three steps is goals. Once you have your goals, you can work backwards to find the method of achieving them. In doing this, you will constantly need to debate the integrity of your intentions as they manifest themselves in means and goals. So, for instance, if what you are really intent upon is finding some way to show that good social practice and behaviour are signs of the kingdom of God, you must be honest about the theological, theistic or even Christocentric intentions which you have. These may not sit easily with other aspects of your beliefs or life-style, such as the acceptance of diversity, or such a belief as the kingdom of God may affect adversely the means or even goals which you espouse. The interaction between the three steps being set out in this chapter is as important as the individual steps themselves. In education this means two things.

Firstly, you need to be careful that you do not try to force children into a pathway to a goal which runs contrary to what they are. Communist or fascist goals are often alluring to those who want clear-cut answers. The damage that is done to individuals and to communities standing in the way of these goals is often horrific. This is why our first step is about our acceptance of the necessity of diversity. Having accepted it, education has to be a part of the process by which, in a democratic fashion, we learn to listen to others' visions of society and goals for society. We must also learn to articulate our visions, our intentions. We need to find out what we disagree about and why: what we have in common and whether what we hold in common means that we actually share final goals; and we have to find ways by which we can handle understandings of our society which are radically different or even totally contradictory to that vision which we have. As Christians we also have to be careful of the two dangers of Christian visions of the future. A very utopian vision ignores that unfashionable word, sin; an apocalyptic vision which dwells too much on sin tends to forget God's love. We need to explore means for discussing and debating the variety of goals in our society.

The second thing which needs to be done is to use the goals as indicators of the process. Take the issue of creativity mentioned above. All major faith systems would agree that creativity, rightly channelled, is an invaluable part of being a human being. Furthermore, all faiths have drawn upon the creative arts for the enhancement and often the spread of their faith. Likewise, secular education and secular society as a whole seem to believe that creativity is an important part of being human. Having said this, we know that we fail most children in our schools and also in our religious communities in that they rarely seem to have the space to use their creativity. There is a gap between our professed agreement on this and the very way we teach, preach, involve people in creative projects or even sponsor creative projects. Is Christianity offering opportunities for creative projects to take place? Does it look at the building of a new church as an opportunity for creative skills in the community to be used? Does it turn to the theatrical and literary worlds when it revises its worship or seeks new liturgies? Is Islam allowing, within the Qur'anic limitations on depicting living beings, the growth of the creative? When did Islam last commission a set of plays or look for new ways of expressing the insights of the faith through architecture? In our schools, do we consult the children on the design of the school, on the layout of the playground — with creative areas as well as games areas for instance? Do we use the skills of the children and their parents in decorating the school or in making a creative contribution to the local area?

Such questions are not academic. They relate to whether we really are willing to unleash previously unused or underused talents and skills. They are about the integrity of what we do and what we say we want. As such they are questions of intention for religious communities as much as for state education.

I believe that Christians in education need to be engaged in these three steps as a vital response to a very dangerous situation. We cannot simply muddle through. We cannot just hang on in there with our schools bearing the names of great saints or missionary figures, and hope that this means they are still "Christian". We cannot rely on Bible studies during lunch breaks or on religious lessons to carry the moral and ethical weight of our systems.

Perhaps storytelling can help us. In discussions created by the Kenya project of Interlink, an interesting model arose — that of life on earth as being the story of God, or God's novel!

In a well-crafted novel, the main story is always a part of a much greater collection of other stories, sub-plots, themes and issues — some of which are relevant to the main story, some of which are not. The skillful writer also knows that a key character does not need to appear all that often. Indeed, some of the best-written novels keep such a character almost entirely out of the story, and the novel consists of our observing the reactions of others to the fact of the existence of the key character. Likewise, the main thrust of a novel can often be carried by a wide range of characters, none really constituting the key person — together they are all the key characters.

Maybe that is how Christians involved in education should see themselves. Possibly, this is how *all* Christians should see themselves. We are part of God's story — God's novel. In the past we behaved as if we had to feature right up-front, on every page of God's novel. We tried to make the entire story, all the plots, themes, characters and heroes, Christian. But what if this is not how the story goes? What if we do only appear every so often in God's story? Perhaps there are other themes of the novel, other stories or sub-stories which God is interested in and our role is to be in relationship to these other stories? For a long time, Christians have been willing to admit that they might not have all the answers! Now I am suggesting that we may not be the only central characters in God's story, and that possibly we need to let other parts of God's story unfold around us in order to find out what our role and purpose in God's story actually is.

It is not just Christians who might benefit from such a model. Educators too might find it helpful, for it asks that we all consider that others might have as significant a role in furthering the story of the world as we do. For Christians engaged in education, asking the sorts of questions explored in earlier chapters, the model of being a part, an important part, but not the whole of God's story could be especially useful. Using a model such as this, look at the three steps outlined earlier in this chapter. In step one, this model theologically calls us to accept diversity — the diversity not just of characters but also story-lines within God's novel of life on earth. However, we are not called to accept just all story-lines or characters. In many stories there are the anti-heroes, the sub-plots which actually threaten the main plot. There are also a number of characters whose role is ambiguous and uncertain. As has been stated above, acceptance of the fact of diversity does not mean accepting that all such diversity is equally good. Far from it. Furthermore, this notion of diverse story-lines should not be seen as meaning just humans. What about the story-lines of the trilobites, the dinosaurs, the great rain forests or the oceans? What right do we have to assume that God is only interested in our part of the story of life?

The second step is means and goals. Using the idea of a novel, of a story, we can perhaps see that there may be a variety of goals and that a good story, precisely because it has a range of characters and plots within it, cannot just have one goal, one "happy ending". It is more complex than that but there will be certain themes or characters which are ultimately of greater importance for the completeness and the wholeness of the story of God. Our quest is to be able to identify such themes and even such characters and to see how we relate to them.

Finally, the integrity of intention. In God's novel, are we acting with integrity of intention? Do we really believe that our role is to be part of a greater whole, or are we secretly hankering after the older model where we, and we alone, hold centre-stage in God's story? To look at life as an unfolding story or stories and to explore our place and role within such a story is to ask ourselves very simple but basic questions. What is my role here? What in the stories I see unfolding around me can I see of God? When am I called to take centre-stage and when am I called to be a supporting figure in such stories? And what, through my faith's teachings and my own journey in faith, do I believe to be God's wish for the story of life on earth? Such questions, honestly explored within a model which contains a critical acceptance of diversity, offer not just a personal quest, but also a framework for Christian understanding of their role within education as well as an understanding of the role of education per se.

I see us as key characters in God's novel. But we are not the only ones. This is not to diminish the Christian role, but to give it a new context. We are never going to "evangelize the world in this generation" nor in the next. What we need to find is a new sense of God's purpose for that part of God's work in history which is called the church. But we must never think that we are the whole story and we sum up God's whole work. We are not even the chief character in God's story.

If the churches can begin to accept this and try to follow the three steps outlined earlier, then we shall have something valid to offer to formal education and to our varied societies. If we don't, and we keep holding to the older models of Christians in education, we may well betray ourselves, our faith and our future.

Some people may feel that this is a rather limiting vision of our role as Christians in education. I do not agree. I believe that the collapse of the older systems and models frees us to be on the cutting edge of both faith and education. There are major issues to which Christians can respond in a way few others can. The insights into the inadequacy of reductionism as a way of understanding the world; the encouragement of creativity; the celebration of God's story of life on earth; the ability to react critically with diversity — all these are vitally necessary for the survival and enhancement of life on earth, and not just human life. Precisely because we can now stop pretending that we run the system or are the dominant culture we can begin to see that the role of Christians in education and in society is to hold in tension the practicalities of education and of society with the vision offered by the Bible of a world living for God.

Christianity can offer models, experiences and insights which are unique and which can help education and pluralism to avoid some of the worse pitfalls of living in a post-certain world — be that post-communist certainty, post-Christian certainty or even post-liberalism certainty. Much which we thought important about our role in society and in education has fallen away or even been taken away. It takes courage to admit this and then to realize that in fact it is a liberation. As such it returns us to the model of the founder of our faith — Jesus Christ, the wandering teacher, with no official post, no qualifications, nowhere to rest his head. But a teacher who taught with authority, who helped others to see for themselves and a teacher who has always travelled with his people of faith into unknown territory and has promised to be with us, even until the end of time.

So let us, as Christians, as educators, as children of God, start to tell God's story anew.